What Holds Europe Together?

Conditions of European Solidarity

What Holds Europe Together?
Volume I

Religion in the New Europe
Volume II

What Holds Europe Together?

Edited by
Krzysztof Michalski

Central European University Press

Budapest   New York

©2006 by Krzysztof Michalski

Published in 2006 by

Central European University Press
An imprint of the
Central European University Share Company
Nádor utca 11, H-1051 Budapest, Hungary
Tel: +36-1-327-3138 or 327-3000
Fax: +36-1-327-3183
E-mail: ceupress@ceu.hu
Website: www.ceupress.com

400 West 59th Street, New York NY 10019, USA
Tel: +1-212-547-6932
Fax: +1-646-557-2416
E-mail: mgreenwald@sorosny.org

ISBN 13: 963 7326 48 0 paperback
ISBN 10: 978-963-7326-48-6

Library of Congress Cataloging-in-Publication Data

Conditions of European solidarity / edited by Krzysztof Michalski.
p. cm.
Contents: v. 1. What holds Europe together?
v. 2 Religion in the new Europe.

1. European federation. 2. European cooperation.
3. Europe—Religion.
I. Michalski, Krzysztof, 1948–

JN15.C595 2005
341.242'2—dc22
2005029454

Printed in Hungary by
Akaprint

Contents

Krzysztof Michalski
Introduction 1

Bronislaw Geremek
Thinking about Europe as a Community 5

Kurt Biedenkopf
"United in Diversity": What Holds Europe Together? 13

Ernst-Wolfgang Böckenförde
Conditions for European Solidarity 30

Heather Grabbe
What Hope for Solidarity in the Enlarged Union? 42

Janos Matyas Kovacs
*Between Resentment and Indifference: Narratives of Solidarity
in the Enlarging Union* 54

Jacques Rupnik
The European Union's Enlargement to the East and Solidarity . . . 86

Kurt Biedenkopf, Bronislaw Geremek, Krzysztof Michalski
and Michel Rocard
What Holds Europe Together? Concluding Remarks 93

COMMENTS
Samuel Abrahám
Needed but Uncertain Cohesion 103

Giuliano Amato
Building Europe 106

Rainer Bauböck
Intersecting and Overlapping European Cultures 112

Ján Čarnogurský
It is Necessary to Believe in Europe 117

Ute Frevert
Does Europe Need a Cultural Identity? Ten Critical Remarks 121

Danuta Hübner
Solidarity on Trial 126

Lech Kaczynski
Europe—Still Divided 131

Ira Katznelson
Reflections on Solidarity 137

Ivan Krastev
Europe's Solidarity Deficit 143

Claus Leggewie
*Turkey's EU Membership as a Litmus Test of European
Self-Confidence* 146

Ulrike Lunacek
European and Global Solidarity 151

Michael Mertes
What Distinguishes Europe? 157

Alexei Miller
European Culture, an Ambivalent Heritage 165

Kenneth Murphy
Solidarity and Freedom 167

Anton Pelinka
Europe is not Europe is not Europe 171

Mykola Riabchuk
Making Barbecue in the European Garden 175

Jan Rokita
Solidarity under Threat 178

Paul Scheffer
Islam in Europe 181

Timothy Snyder
United Europe, Divided History 185

List of Contributors 189

KRZYSZTOF MICHALSKI

Introduction

The European Union is facing a great challenge, perhaps its greatest thus far. On the one hand, it is expanding on a dramatic scale: over 70 million more people will have EU passports in the near future. On the other hand, the EU is attempting to radically redefine itself through the process of drawing up a Constitution and by metamorphosing into a new kind of political union.

Enlargement brings people into the Union who are often much poorer than, and culturally very different from, most of its existing citizens. Economic and cultural divergences within the Union will widen dramatically and reflect greater contrasts as a result. At the same time, the process of drawing up the Constitution is an attempt to redefine the unity of the Union in a more ambitious way. What could hold the European Union together in this situation, where growing diversity goes hand in hand with unity of a more demanding nature? What values, traditions and aims can bring Lithuanians and Basques, Polish farmers and Scottish miners together in a single democratic structure, thereby strengthening and solidifying the future European Constitution?

The contributions to the present volumes examining the *Conditions of European Solidarity* concentrate on a few specific areas that may be sore issues in the process of European integration. One of them is, of course, the enlargement of the Union to include the countries of the former Soviet empire. How will this enlargement alter the conditions of European solidarity? What will these new members bring to the family table? Will they—as many fear—be no more than spoilsports, poor, dirty, unenlightened fellows with questionable democratic traditions (if, indeed, they have any such traditions in the first place)? Will they slow down the process of the Union's democratization, or even bring it to a halt? Will they put a stop to a common foreign policy and destroy heaven knows what other precious assets— just as they (some people claim) are ruining the labor market? Or might it be that they will not only expose the Union to new risks, but also create new opportunities? 1989 ushered in a sea change for Europe. Does that year live on in our actions, or has it become a mere museum piece? "Solidarity," after all, was the slogan of the 1989 revolution. Are there other lessons to be drawn from the solidarity of the past for the solidarity we need today?

In the revolutionary 1980s the name "Solidarity"—first in Poland, then, quickly taking on a well-nigh-mythical status in other countries as well—stood for a social bond uniting people independently of existing political institutions. This bond proved to be the basis for a radical and vital reform of the political order—indeed, a revolution. It was proven that genuine political realism needed to take this reality, rather than merely the interests articulated in the "real existing" political institutions, on board.

The solidarity of these years offers an experience from which today's Europeans still could learn. Another lesson of 1989 is that it is hardly possible to address the issue of social identity without examining the dimension of the future—that is, people's wishes, expectations and dreams, of which they are often only dimly aware. Sometimes these wishes and dreams can be mobilized to achieve a large shared project—such as that of a free society, in 1989. Today, that project might be Europe itself.

The issue of Europe's religions is of particular interest in this context. After European solidarity it is the second main topic of this collection. Having learned from their tragic experiences, Europe's democratic societies have sought over the last two centuries to oust religion from the political sphere. It was not for nothing that it was viewed as a source of contention, rather than unity. This is certainly still often the case today. However, it may be that European religions also have the potential to bring the people of Europe closer together, instead of dividing them further. The contributions to the second volume take a close look at this issue. Particular attention is paid to the role of Islam in the European public sphere.

In the spring of 2002, the then President of the European Commission, Romano Prodi, asked the *Institut für die Wissenschaften vom Menschen* (IWM, Institute for Human Sciences) in Vienna to set up a group of Europeans to reflect on those values particularly relevant to the continuing process of European unification and to advise him on this field. The individuals involved, he requested, should be independent persons, not representatives of political parties, churches or other organizations; they should possess intellectual credentials, political experience and a non-partisan stature in their countries. Over the next, few weeks the group was set up and soon began work.[1] With the European Commission's support, the group repeatedly met with experts on the relevant issues. Additionally, in order to involve as broad a swathe of the general public as possible from the very outset, rather than presenting a *fait accompli*, the Group has held a series of public debates in several European capitals.[2] Under the general title *Conditions of European Solidarity* the two volumes *What Holds Europe together?* and *Religion in the New Europe* present the main outcomes of the group's meetings and public debates.[3]

In the concluding remarks "What Holds Europe Together?" (vol. 1, pp. 93–102) four members of the Reflection Group summarize the central ideas developed during its work. This "Europe Paper" was then circulated to a number of scholars, intellectuals and politicians from Europe, East and West, and the United States for comments (see ibid, pp. 103–188).

We hope that the reflections presented in these volumes can provide fresh impetus to the debate on the new union of Europe.

Notes

[1] Its members were: Kurt Biedenkopf, Silvio Ferrari, Bronislaw Geremek, Árpád Göncz, John Gray, Will Hutton, Jutta Limbach, Krzysztof Michalski, Ioannis Petrou, Alberto Quadrio Curzio, Michel Rocard and Simone Veil. Further details are available at: www.iwm.at/r-reflec.htm and http://europa. eu.int/comm/research/social-sciences/group/michalski_en.htm.

[2] The first of these (organized in cooperation with the Warsaw-based Stefan Batory Foundation) was held in the residence of the Polish President in Warsaw; the second (organized in cooperation with the Austrian Industrialists' Association) took place in Prince Schwarzenberg's palace in Vienna, while

the third and fourth were held in Paris (in cooperation with *La République des idées* and hosted by Dominique de Villepin, at that time French Minister for Foreign Affairs) and Berlin (hosted by de Villepin's German counterpart, Joschka Fischer).

Another means of bringing the ideas of the group to the attention of a broader cross-section of the European public were newspaper columns written by the members on the topics under discussion. These were published in cooperation with *Project Syndicate*, a non-commercial international group of more than 250 daily newspapers in Europe and beyond. Twelve columns have appeared in 49 newspapers and 32 countries.

[3] They were first published in German in IWM's journal *Transit— Europäische Revue*, nr. 26, 27 and 28 (Verlag Neue Kritik, Frankfurt a.M., 2003/ 2004).

BRONISLAW GEREMEK

Thinking about Europe as a Community

Jean Monnet is supposed to have said that if he were to start again, he would begin with culture. We know that he never did say that because he—the inspiration behind European integration—knew very well that in that case he would have failed. Others say that this process should have begun with politics; but there too, failure would have been inevitable. European integration had to begin with the economy, but its future now depends on the European Union making a success of its efforts to lend itself a political dimension. And it is now that the challenge we can describe as cultural arises, although it goes well beyond heritage or cultural policy. It is more about the big questions: Where do we come from? Where are we? Where are we going?

Thinking about Europe in terms of political unity—or even *as* a specific political unit—means thinking about its values, its memory, its traditions, even of the will of its citizens to live together. The challenges facing Europe at the beginning of the twenty-first century require a profound change in the European discourse. We must abandon the language of accountants and go back to the language of day-to-day communication, where we ask ourselves what is good or bad, beautiful or ugly, right or wrong. At the current turning point in the European Union's history, it is not only that Community institutions need to be redefined, but also that a feeling of belonging to the Community needs to be generated.

The work that has been done in the constitutional field of European Union's legislative process—I am thinking of the European Treaties and of the Charter of Fundamental Rights and of the European Constitution—clearly demonstrates how awareness of growing Community feeling, of an "ever more united Europe," is moving forward step by step. But it is eastward enlargement, attesting to the end of the Cold War and ending the division of Europe into two blocs, which has made the prospect of a unified Europe a reality. The Convention on the Future of Europe created by the Laeken Declaration and presided over with admirable skill by Valéry Giscard d'Estaing was part of this drive towards European unification. Its importance is measured not only by its immediate result—the draft constitutional treaty (or constitution—the term has become acceptable even to the British)—but also by the fact that it has had an impact on European public opinion and launched the broadest European debate to date. It is here—and not in the wave of pacifism that emerged in the face of the Iraq war—that we are witnessing the gestation of a truly European public space. The future of the European Union most definitely depends on the institutional reforms that will come of it. But it also depends on the debate as to what the European idea really means.

The debate on "union" must now be accompanied by a debate on "community." The beginning of this debate on community can be seen in the work of the Convention on the Charter of Fundamental Rights (chaired by Roman Herzog); but in spite of this document having been publicly disseminated it has not had an impact on public opinion. The Convention on the Future of Europe has been only marginally involved in this debate—while it was working on the preamble of the constitution. It is of no value simply to rue missed opportunities.

If European integration is to progress, we must now overcome the national egoisms which appear in the interplay between governments and call on feelings of shared belonging that go beyond national sentiment. I believe that "a federation of nation states" accurately describes the current nature of the European Union and attests to the fact that the diversity of national cultures is—and, in my view, will remain—Europe's richest resource. But meanwhile, the national egoisms that are always present in the horse-trading routine of the EU's summits and in intergovernmental negotiations, are its shame. There was a joke in the Risorgimento (the period of the formation of Italian unity): "we have created Italy; now we must create Italians." Likewise, we could say that now that we have Europe, we need Europeans. In other words, we need to think of Europe as a community.

First of all, let us say that this does not necessarily occur automatically. The history of national feeling shows us how difficult and con-flictual the process of developing national awareness was, even though it was founded on the feeling of a common destiny and sites of shared memory, and on a common language and culture. The community bond was the fruit of a long accumulation of experience and knowledge, with an entire mythological and historical construction lending it an organic character. There is nothing comparable in the case of the Euro-pean bond, which seems the result of a deliberate choice, rather than an organic process of evolution.

When we talk about problems of collective psychology, attitudes and sentiments, future plans and choices of culture (or civilization), we inevitably need to look back at history on the one hand, and val-ues—i.e. axiology—on the other.

*

The feeling of belonging, or of European identity, can be considered in terms of different strands of experience.

First of all, within the weft of European history there has been a series of attempts at imperial unification, all characterized by a respect for ethnic differences and individual sovereignties within the Empire. The old medieval principle declaring that the king is emperor within his kingdom can be understood as the expression of this state of affairs: it sufficed to accept the unity of the empire and the power of the emperor in order to enjoy individual freedom. There were sometimes significant differences between imperial policies. Charlemagne saw the Christian-ization of the Saxons as a necessary precondition to their submission to his power; the Ottomans, successors to the Byzantine empire, expect-ed nothing from the subject peoples except taxes and tributes—not the abandonment of their faith; Charles V, in his empire on which "the sun never set," supported Catholicism but was persuaded to accept religious schisms; Napoleon accepted all religions, with the religion of liberty taking pride of place, and accepted all nations, with the Grande Nation at their head, while nonetheless expecting their full submission to the imperial power. The empires saw themselves not only as superior powers but also, above all, as what the Germans call a *Rechtsordnung*, a legal order. The Holy Roman Empire of the Germanic nation in the Middle Ages imposed a legal framework in which the monarchies and

principalities of the time found both a space where they could coexist
and rules of administration. The Civil Code carried by the bayonets
of Napoleon's troops throughout Europe (and which left its mark on
property or contract law in countries like Poland right up to the present day) could be applied in various political and cultural environ-
ments. These legal orders were in no way communities of values. In
fact, rather the opposite: they preserved the authorities' and citizens'
rights independently of the community of values to which they belonged,
even without any relation to the fundamental values which they advo-
cated, as long as they obeyed the law.

We could limit the European Union's prospects to this experience
of imperial unification and conclude, as did the German philosopher
Robert Spaemann, that Europe can only become a community of law
with all citizens of countries with a European tradition under a common roof when it enables communities sharing value judgments to
exist in security, and when it renounces the aim of becoming a community of values. I do not think that we can use the term community
to refer to these "imperial moments" in Europe's history. In the legal
order, imposition predominates over participation; the citizen is subject to obligations imposed and rights granted. It would be difficult to
see how this path leads us to the realization of the "purpose" of the
European Union, or to any kind of reference point for the current process
of European unification.

Equally significant to the current debate are the periods of unification in the history of Europe. First and foremost comes medieval
Christianity in its 13th-century form. At its head was the emperor and
the pope, ensuring cooperation between spiritual and temporal power,
pursuing the "Latin" tradition whereby the Church preserved its sovereignty over the state within the Western world while the Byzantine
Church fell under its domination. This community was united around
a similar faith and its unifying power had a center, Rome, where the
successors of Saint Peter had their seat. It also contained a network of
universities that were part of the Church, disseminating knowledge
and educating the cultural elites in the same way and using the same
language (Latin), as well as a network of churches built in the same
style throughout Europe, using the same calendar and the same liturgy.
Medieval Christianity was by nature European, although it avoided the
word itself (it was only taken up again by the great humanist—and

pope—Enea Silvio Piccolomini in the 15th century) and accepted all national forms of cultural expression.

The second community period in the history of Europe (until the Enlightenment and its flourishing of vernacular languages, with French prime among them) is Erasmus' "Republic of Letters"—with Latin still the language of communication. The religious discourse that initially dominated this intellectual movement gave way to observation and analysis of the world, with unlimited faith in scientific progress and the force of reason. The natural framework for this community was Europe: the common spirit was served by a communications network that allowed rapid dissemination of ideas and writings despite the technological limitations of the time. Intellectual and cultural ties were reinforced by travel, which provided knowledge of the whole of Europe, and brought the continent closer together. From the pen of these citizens of the Republic of Letters, such constructions as "we Europeans" or Montesquieu's statement that "Europe is just one nation made up of many" flowed naturally.

The reason I have chosen to present these two community experiences in this short paper is because together they can be considered the key reference point for a European identity. Both cases were about the formation of communities, but in pursuit of opposite ends. Karl Jaspers, speaking on the European spirit in Geneva in 1946, declared that European liberty was founded on antitheses. "Europe," he said, "brings together opposite extremes: the secular world and transcendence, science and faith, material technology and religion." We should also insist that the European Union not be afraid to refer both to the community of medieval Christianity and the community of reason of the modern era, because in this way it will be able to affirm the contradictory essence of the European spirit. And thus justice is done to history.

There must be a place for religion in Europe's constitutional documents. Thus, in the Maastricht Treaty, we find the "ecclesiastical clause" proposed by Helmut Kohl, ensuring respect for the status of all churches and confessional communities. In the text of the Constitution drawn up by the Convention, there are clear guarantees of the status of the churches and religious institutions in national legislation and an affirmation of the need for regular dialogue between the authorities of the Union and the churches (Article 51). These legal provisions should go hand in hand with the Declaration of Individual and Collective Freedom of Religion included in the Charter of Fundamental Rights. However, the debate on the preamble gave rise to significant conflicts. First we refused to mention Europe's religious heritage, then we forgot to talk about Christianity or the Judeo-Christian heritage and cited only the Enlightenment tradition alongside the Greeks and Romans. The compromise solution that was provisionally accepted carries a weak, indeed obscure message. And that is a pity.

We could of course drop the preamble so as not to create conflict on a delicate subject. Over the course of its history, Europe has paid a painful price for its religious conflicts and rifts. We should do everything to avoid rekindling these feuds. If we consider that the constitutional treaty must not only introduce more clarity, transparency and efficiency into the workings of the European institutions, but also bring the European Union closer to its citizens, we need to introduce a bit of "European metaphysics." We need to talk about the European idea and the European spirit so that the text can encourage the citizens of Europe to think about how we came together, why we are staying together and what we want to do together. It is in this way that the document could become a tool for a European education—in schools and in life.

I have only looked at the vicissitudes of the work on the Constitution in order to illustrate the importance of the debate as to Europe's history and values. It is this debate that enables us to identify those common traits in European civilization to which both religious and secular traditions contributed.

If we apply "the work of memory"—a concept dear to Paul Ricœur— to Europe, we find how Europe's identity in the Middle Ages was bound up with a unifying Christian faith and, in early modern times, by the unifying confidence in the power of reason. We also see how agreement was reached on ethical principles defining human behaviors and attitudes, although disagreement remained as to the source of these principles. Finally, we arrive at the fundamental values that Europe chose for itself as the foundation on which to construct a Promethean community of freedom and solidarity. It seems to me that we cannot confine ourselves to making an inventory of the different heritages bequeathed to Europe, since history creates choices and possibilities but does not distribute them; though it forms civilizations and societies it does not restrict them to moulds set in stone. For Europe to advance it must, at every decisive moment in its history, ask itself what it is about.

The answer seems to revolve around the place that our European civilization has given to the human person since mixing barbarian customs with Christianity. This anthropocentric vision is carried by Christian tradition in the message that man is made in the image of God and that the Son of God sacrificed himself for man. But we also find it in the non-religious tradition, which declares that man is the measure of all things or (cf. Pico della Mirandola) that he is vested with grandeur and dignity. What is important is that this anthropocentrism is rooted as much in the Judeo-Christian tradition as in a humanist philosophy of man. All the values which the different communities draw on—and which the European Union now refers to—are rooted in this specific value. It is human dignity that is the source of human liberty, notions of justice, solidarity or freedom of choice, and human rights. The dual foundation of European anthropocentrism makes it possible to transcend the conflict between religion and secularism that accompanied the recent discussion on the ideological bases of the Constitution. It can also be the starting point for a genuine debate on the future of Europe, by using the model of a civilization and the project of a community that puts man and his dignity in a central position.

Let us briefly take a closer look at three questions concerning the way Europe works as a community of values. First of all, community values should not be seen as a partition closing off access to the community. Introducing axiology into the political arena carries with it the risk of a tendency towards the absolute, which could generate attitudes and policies of exclusion. We must avoid ethnocentric tendencies that exclude others. The concept of human dignity must encourage dialogue with the Other and a radical opening towards others in the sense called for by Emmanuel Levinas. Europe owes it to itself to be pluralist, aware of its debt to the Greeks and the Romans, the Arabs and the Jews in terms of the handing down of culture. It needs to learn from its own experience the power of tolerance and the poverty of closed, totalitarian ideologies that throw a shadow of shame over Europe.

Secondly, human rights policy must define the very image of Europe; it must be its emblem or even its "religion." This applies to the European Union's internal politics in the same way that the "Copenhagen criteria" lay down the primary conditions for accession. Human

rights should be the ideological benchmark for European foreign policy—otherwise the creation of the post of EU foreign affairs minister
will remain a dead letter. In the current situation it is very important
that Europe should be able to base the multilateralism of its foreign
policy on human rights, while at the same time working on reforming
international law and the UN system to ensure that human rights win
out over shortsighted political calculations. How otherwise can the
system and its laws be defended?

Thirdly, we also need to rethink the model of European development within this "personalist" perspective. In France, as the *Ancien
Régime* was coming to an end, the Committee of Mendicancy formed
within the Constituent Assembly declared: "We have always thought
to give charity to the poor, but never to assert the poor man's rights
vis-à-vis society or society's rights vis-à-vis him." This revealing statement not only illustrates the power of the human rights syndrome, but
also puts the problem of poverty in the perspective of modern social
policies. It also encourages discussion of the European social model,
not around issues of acquired rights, but around the social dialogue,
responding to the requirements of human dignity and incorporating
the program of the ATD Fourth World movement into the European
project.

The remedies for European malaise must not concern only the
institutions and policies; they must also galvanize ideas. Calls for the
formation of a "hard core" of European integration are inappropriate
when the most important thing is to strengthen European solidarity.
Exploiting an unfavorable view of Americans in order to define Europe
in opposition to something negative—just as the Athenians defined
themselves in opposition to the Persians or the Europeans in relation
to the Arabs, Tartars or Turks—is a strategy that destroys the chances
of Europe emerging on the international scene as a useful partner. The
role of the intellectual debate on the future of Europe is to go "beyond
the pillars of Hercules," to produce ideas and visions that would be
powerful enough to show realistically what direction to take and to
mobilize the imagination to build a powerful, courageous and lucid
Europe.

KURT BIEDENKOPF

"United in diversity": What Holds Europe Together?

Conscious that Europe is a continent that has brought forth civilization; that its inhabitants ... have gradually developed the values underlying humanism: equality of persons, freedom, respect for reason,

Drawing inspiration from the cultural, religious and humanist
inheritance of Europe...

Believing that reunited Europe intends to continue along the path
of civilization, progress and prosperity, for the good of all its inhabitants ... that it wishes to remain a continent open to culture, learning
and social progress; and that it wishes ... to strive for peace, justice
and solidarity throughout the world,

Convinced that, while remaining proud of their own national identities and history, the peoples of Europe are determined to transcend
their ancient divisions and, united ever more closely, to forge a common destiny,

Convinced that, thus "united in its diversity," Europe offers them
the best chance of pursuing, with due regard for the rights of each individual and in awareness of their responsibilities towards future generations and the Earth, the great venture which makes of it a special area
of human hope...

It is in this somewhat lofty language that the Preamble to the draft
Treaty establishing a Constitution for Europe describes the foundations
of the Community of states and peoples who have banded together in
the European Union to set about shaping their joint future. The draft
here sets out the goals and values, which it hopes, will give meaning
and lasting stability to the continuing process of European integration and the building of a political union.

To consider the objectives and values that could be said to form the intellectual foundation of the Union, to define them and examine their solidity, is one of the objectives of the reflection group that Romano Prodi set up in Brussels in January 2003. The President of the European Commission felt that, in parallel to the work of the Constitutional Convention, there was a need to take stock of the spiritual and cultural dimension of an enlarged Europe, and to look for answers to the questions, "Who are we? From what roots does a shared certainty of belonging together grow?" Prodi's concern has been to identify and think through the fundamental principles that provide the basis on which all the citizens of the European Union can live together. New rules of coexistence, he believes, can be used to create a real community of peoples and civil society in a Europe living in freedom with its neighbors. Prodi feels that, if the debate on the Constitutional Treaty is to clarify the basis on which the new political unit, the Union, is to rest, it must turn on the interrelations between scales of values, politics and European citizenship. When we look to the future of Europe, we cannot confine ourselves to the Union's economic achievements and ignore its spiritual, religious and ethical dimensions.

In avowing his conviction as to the importance of these dimensions, President Prodi is acknowledging that the state cannot itself establish the foundations on which it rests. What is true of the state is just as true of the European Union. It cannot by itself create the prerequisites that would make it a unit that can be defined in a constitution. For that, it must depend on other sources, and on other strengths. These include common values, a shared cultural and historical background, and common interests, ambitions and challenges. It is these characteristics above all that help to establish a community and hold it together. They are the foundations of its identity.

These characteristics also make Europe capable of giving substance and life to a constitution. They provide an indication of its capacity to act, of its solidity and, thus, of its ability to overcome tensions and crises with the strength of community: in short, of its ability to endure as an entity unified in diversity.

The considerations I will be outlining here start out from the overriding question, "What holds Europe together, and what will hold it together now that it is to be a Union of 25 European states?" Starting from this question allows the task of the Constitutional Treaty to be circumscribed. Constitutional questions are also questions of values; but any attempt to provide a constitution for a community assumes that the community already exists. The constitution as such cannot provide that identity. This was seen, for example, after the foundation of the Federal Republic of Germany in 1949, when an attempt was made to provide the Federal Republic with an identity apprehended by its citizens. This concept of a patriotism centered on a constitution, put forward by Dolf Sternberger, came to nothing. A constitutional framework can only envelop that which already exists as a unit that can be expressed in a constitution, and which aspires to such a goal.

The draft Constitutional Treaty currently being discussed and decided upon, however, gives us an opportunity to measure the work of the Convention against criteria that are not intrinsic to a constitution, but rather relate to its prerequisites. As far as I am aware, the Convention did not concern itself greatly with these prerequisites: it considered them givens. Whether that assumption was justified is the point of the question, "What holds the European Union together?"

We will also be looking at the draft to see whether, and in what contexts, the spiritual and cultural dimensions addressed by President Prodi are reflected in the actual text of the constitution, especially the goals it sets out, and how the constitutional dimension relates to the pre-constitutional one.

I

First, however, we have to ask, "What has held the European Union together in the approximately 50 years of its existence? Can we assume that the same forces of cohesion will continue to operate in future? What forces can take their place when, as the European Union develops, they exhaust their present strength or, in any event, lose their significance?"

In the early decades of European integration, from the European Economic Community of the Rome Treaties to the European Union of the 1980s and the early 1990s, several political forces ensured inner cohesion. To begin with, there was a longing for peace in Europe, and for a life worthy of free human beings. The fact that, in the first half of the twentieth century, Europe had nearly succeeded in destroying itself, coupled with the horrors of the Nazi regime, generated a common will and determination among Europeans to do whatever was necessary to prevent a repetition of a European civil war and a renewed threat to human rights. The inner unification of Europe was the only conceivable path to this objective. The determination to take that path was so great that, just a few years after the end of the war, Europe had already overcome the urge for reprisal and revenge against Germany.

The desire for European unity was encouraged by the common threat emanating from Communism and the Soviet Union. That threat led to the foundation of NATO, and thus to a defense community that included both the United States and the free part of Germany. The Atlantic Community and its clear defensive role also established a bond between the founder members of the European Economic Community, a bond that was stronger than the differences of opinion and clashes of interest that continued to exist after the EEC had been set up.

Partly as a result of the protection provided by the United States, the European Economic Community was able to concentrate more intensively on the joint reconstruction of a Europe still in ruins. Even the Coal and Steel Community was not intended only to prevent the emergence of new national arms industries. It also sought to lay the foundations for the reconstruction of industry. After the attempt at political integration foundered in the French National Assembly in 1954, economic integration became the accepted approach to European integration.

Along with economic integration went the expectation of a steadily rising standard of living. In the 1970s the expectation of prosperity solidified into a promise of growth. It has continued to be a determining factor in economic policy in Europe, as it is in all highly developed industrial countries.

These elemental forces—a longing for peace, a striving for freedom, defense against a common threat, a determination to rebuild and a promise of prosperity—gave direction and meaning to the drive for integration. They reinforced the spiritual, cultural, historical and religious bonds between the Member States of the Union. But they were tied to a particular time. As goals they are still there, but the unifying force they contributed to the development of the European Union has faded.

This is true above all of the threat from the East, which had died away by the end of the Cold War. To the generations of Europeans now shaping the future, peace and freedom are a matter of course: no special effort is called for to achieve them, and no special effort can be justified by invoking them. With the unification of Germany and Europe, if not before, the common threat from the East was overcome. The Soviet Union is no more. Communist rule has defeated itself.

The Russia that has emerged within new frontiers maintains close relations with NATO. The former Soviet satellite states are now members of the former defensive alliance. The old NATO is gone. It is true that recent terrorist actions have brought new dangers for Europe. But so far there is no unequivocal threat to all the Member States that could generate an awareness of an immediate common danger, and a need for common defensive measures. The new dangers may unite us, but they may just as easily divide us.

The joint construction of the European Union by its old Member States is essentially complete. The Union has been knit into an economic and currency union. The integration of its economies has progressed so far that a new separation into independent national economies is inconceivable. The existence of a common market is taken for granted. The original objective of the European Economic Community has been achieved.

Safeguarding and developing that common market will go on being one of the European Union's constant concerns. But the Union will also face new economic and social challenges. Markets are expanding beyond its borders and worldwide. Expanding markets are opening up not just new economic opportunities, but also new risks and forms of dependence. The concept of globalization may not explain them, but it does serve as a convenient way to sum them up. Economic growth and the improvement of living standards have fallen behind the levels sought after. The promise that rising unemployment in the European Union would be overcome has, thus far, not been fulfilled. To the great majority of Europeans it seems unlikely that it will be fulfilled in the foreseeable future. Everywhere social security systems are straining the limits of what can be financed, and this is unleashing new uncertainties.

Enlargement brings further difficulties. Some 75 million Europeans who will vote in elections to the European Parliament for the first time next year are pinning their hopes and expectations on entry to the European Union, a goal that can be met at best within a generation. Their accession will accentuate the East–West prosperity divide within the Union. The inequality among the citizens of the Union is only bound to grow. The accession of the ten central and south-eastern European states will bring difficulties of adaptation and conversion which, in the eyes of many, will outweigh the benefits of enlargement, at least in the next few years.

These new uncertainties, burdens and dangers originate in part within the European Union itself. In part they are the consequence of the paradigm shift from the industrial age to the age of knowledge, the worldwide interlinking of markets, and of demographic trends in Europe, the Mediterranean area and the world in general. Demographic developments in particular will change the face of Europe in the coming decades. In all Member States the birth rate is below the level that would be needed to renew the population. Some of the lowest rates are to be found in Poland, Germany, Spain and Italy. At the same time, people's life expectancy is increasing. The generations already born as well as the future generations—for whose well-being, according to the Preamble to the draft Constitution, Europe is responsible—will have to bear burdens that, in their social and personal dimensions, will go beyond anything previously experienced in peacetime.

What political and social tensions the demographic revolution may generate is difficult to assess. It will certainly call for profound changes in our thinking and in our political and social structures; it will severely test our values. The foreseeable migrations from weaker to stronger regions inside Europe will hold back the development prospects of the weaker areas. This will lead to demands on the Union that will certainly not always be compatible with the "area of freedom, security and justice" referred to in Article 3 of the draft Constitution. It is surprising, therefore, that the draft Constitution takes no real notice, as far as I can see, of these predictable developments and their significance for the Union's internal cohesion.

II

To get an idea of what sort of cohesive forces there will have to be in the European Union in order to hold Europe together in future, at a time when thoroughgoing changes are and will be taking place, we must consider what new problems we can expect it to face, and what forces of cohesion we can hope to be able to rely on.

First, the new challenges and burdens. These will arise out of the enlargement of the European Union, the effects of the demographic trends already described, the changes in the economy and the labor market, the consequences of globalization for the citizens and their environment, and the paradigm shift from the industrial age to the age of knowledge.

All of the Member States of the European Union will be forced in the next few years to privatize their social welfare systems, to extend the sphere of the citizen's own responsibility, to confine state payments to the provision of basic needs, and thus to protect the state from the self-destructive effects of a constant expansion in its responsibilities to its citizens. The public will see the measures this will require as negative and as a breach of social welfare commitments, until such time as they have been convinced that the changes will benefit them in the long term and that to try to continue as before will lead nowhere.

All Member States will face political challenges of much the same kind, challenges for which, after some thirty years of social welfare and redistributive policies, or a similarly long period within the socialist guardian state, they are not prepared. Smaller Member States will have less difficulty taking on this task than larger ones.

The enlargement of the European Union will place new burdens on the 15 existing Member States. But it will also increase strains among the 25. Europe will have to live for decades with greater inequality between the living standards and prosperity of the people of its Member States. In Europe there has always been a prosperity divide between East and West. During the division of the continent, this divide merely widened. But in the "old" Union it had no great political effect. With the unification of Germany and Europe, those strong differences have become much clearer. They can be overcome, if at all, only over time-scales measured in generations.

Inequalities in prosperity between regions within independent States having their own national identity can be accepted and tolerated with relatively little difficulty. But with EU entry and the extension of European rules to the Eastern and Central European accession nations, the barriers that previously made comparisons difficult will be swept away. People in the eastern and south-eastern parts of the continent will begin to take Western levels of prosperity as their yardstick. Just how difficult it will be to convince them that there will necessarily be a long road to travel before they attain standards comparable to those in the West is evident from the German experience. Those concerned, even when it may be unavoidable, will see wider inequality as an injustice, once the old borders have gone and the comparisons that were once impossible begin to be made. The threshold of tolerance will be lowered still further by the transparency of living conditions in the Union that is created by the media.

Anyone concerning themselves with "values" will have to answer the questions of how wider inequality in the enlarged EU can be politically justified, given the goal of equality between citizens, and of how such inequality may affect the inner cohesion of the EU. Here, we have to understand these values in terms of the economic and social coloring now given to them. This is true especially of solidarity and equality. Equality is now primarily taken to mean equality of economic living conditions, rather than equality before the law.

That inequalities between Eastern and Western Europe might be offset in the same way as equalities between eastern and western Germany is not to be expected. The European Union would have to earmark some 4% of its GDP for annual transfer payments for many years to come. The new Member States do not possess the infrastructure—political, economic, social and administrative—that they would need to be able to handle such transfers. In the enlarged European Union there is inevitably going to be wide and continuing inequality for a long time.

As already mentioned, this may lead to greater East–West mobility in the section of the population whose abilities are in demand in Western Europe. As a rule, these are people who are badly needed for the development of their own countries. Demographic development will reinforce this trend. The full effect of the demographic upheaval will be felt at just about the time the new members become fully integrated into the Union. The Member States will be competing for the elites from "baby-bust" age groups. As the German example illustrates, individual regions' interest in further economic and scientific development will usually be stronger than any attempt to cater to the development prospects of weaker regions on a nationwide basis. When it comes to relations between Member States, the stronger regions' desire for development will be tempered even less by considerations of solidarity and common interest. This position is unlikely to be greatly changed by the insistent calls for solidarity within the Union within the Constitutional Treaty and on the part of the political leadership.

The existing inequality is also not likely to be narrowed by economic growth. Quite to the contrary, sustained economic growth in the EU can only be expected to accentuate it. The fact that EU policy has been strongly oriented towards economic growth has always been problematic. But as long as the economies inside the common market were relatively comparable, the strains created by divergent development could be dealt with. This will change in future. To form an idea of the scale of this growth in inequality, one has to measure economic growth, not in percentages of GDP, but in absolute figures. If percentage growth rates are roughly similar, the inequality due to the different points of departure will grow steadily wider. This also can be seen from the German–German case. A growth-oriented economic policy is worth pursuing, but the promise of growth is not likely to act as a force for cohesion in the enlarged EU.

Higher rates of growth in the economically stronger Member States will tend, instead, to strengthen the centrifugal forces in the Union. Nor is it to be expected that the strains this will cause can be reduced or removed by transfer payments from the strong to the weak Member States. Experience to date has shown that there is just as little to be hoped from the possibility that the EU might relax its system of rules, the *acquis communautaire*, so as to allow the weaker Member States to offset their economic weakness by means of greater freedom of organization (subsidiarity) and innovation. Compensatory arrangements of this kind did not work in Germany either.

What is true of the promise of growth is also true of the promise of social welfare and solidarity, for two reasons. The weaker states, especially the new ones, will find that to extend their social systems on the Western model is beyond their capabilities and will certainly lead to ruin. They will therefore have to look for European support and solidarity. People in the strong Member States, on the other hand, will have to cut back social welfare demands on the state and take over part of the responsibility for their social risks themselves. But this necessity will be dictated, not by considerations of responsible freedom and civil society, but by the threatened insolvency of the state. This justification is also questionable in other respects, but it is not likely to encourage a readiness in stronger states to show solidarity with the weak in any event. Here too the scene is set for new tensions.

What held the EU together in the past, then, will not hold it together in the same way in future. In some cases the old forces of cohesion are exhausted, and in others the foundations on which they rested have disappeared. The orientation of European integration towards economic, social and financial policy is not by itself enough to bind Europe together: the earlier promises of growth and social welfare can no longer be fulfilled because the desired results cannot be achieved. The causes of economic and social tension in Europe—an overburdened state, mounting inequality, demographic developments and globalization will strengthen the trend towards regional mediation of economic and social interests, towards competition between regions— will, in fact, increase.

III

This shift will not threaten the EU's inner cohesion if other cohesive forces can be mobilized and promoted. But these forces would have to be strong enough to counter the strains caused by continued inequality, competition between regions and within the economy of the EU and the burdens of change. Given the situation, such forces will not be generated primarily by the EU's economic and social objectives. Neither the European economic and monetary union nor a European labor market and social policy will have the peacemaking and identity-building effect being spoken of here. The EU must have recourse to forces capable of overcoming inner tensions and new challenges, forces that can provide a foundation for cohesion and for European identity independently of economic and social developments. But these new cohesive forces must be sought essentially in the non-economic sector.

Towards the end of his life, Jean Monnet is reported to have said that, if he had to begin again, he would begin with culture. He may have been right, but that idea is not easy to put into practice. There can be no serious doubt as to Europe's cultural unity. The West is marked by its Christian religion, its cultural and spiritual heritage, and its common history. But culture and religion have not been determining forces in public life for some time. As public life has become secularized and increasingly centered on the economy, while life in society has been largely individualized, culture and religion have become a private, individual matter and, to a great extent, have lost their power to act as the foundation of a community and an identity. Their place has been taken by the economy, science and technology, the market, and state-imposed solidarity.

In the United States there is a cohesive force in the form of the nation which transcends the economic to give meaning to the whole, but this would not be possible in Europe if only because there is not going to be a European nation. The United States is a continent united by a nation; Europe is a continent with a multiplicity of nations. European integration aims to transcend the nation state. The nation can therefore be ruled out as a common denominator for Europe.

It seems quite plain to me that, in order to exist as a political entity, the EU must attach greater importance to what it has in common culturally, in the broadest sense of the word. This will mean that cultural institutions will take on a new political meaning. What we are saving on armies as a result of peace in Europe we should, in order to secure European unity, be investing in education and training, research and development, and in the culture of Europe and its Member States. What people are saving on the cost of bringing up children as a result of demographic developments and the falling birth rate, should be channeled into the education of succeeding generations, and into the building of a stock of capital that will enable those succeeding generations, fewer in number and better educated, to create a standard of living as high as that which the present population of Europe aspires to, or takes for granted.

The languages of Europe are an intrinsic component of Europe's identity. They cannot be unified without destroying culture as a force

for political cohesion. The common European language is European
culture and its emanations in music, literature, painting, sculpture,
design and architecture, which are seen by all as European, embody-
ing a European identity. It is this identity whose care, protection and
defense must be, and remain, a European responsibility.

This does not mean that there cannot be a general language of
day-to-day contact in Europe, a *lingua franca* used alongside the many
other languages as a more or less technical form of communication
in particular fields. Business and finance, the natural sciences and
other specialized areas will make use of standard specialized languages.
But such languages have a limited capacity to act as the foundation
of identity. They will not reach much beyond their particular specialized area, and it would be dangerous to assume otherwise. One can
use a *lingua franca* to describe tears, but not to describe their causes.

It is important to realize that the cultural dimension of a European
identity holding Europe together cannot simply be created by state
action. The state can join with the institutions of society to underpin
the substance, the development and the care of its cultural heritage,
and of contemporary culture in the widest sense. But it cannot enforce
a cultural identity. In this respect, whether Europe holds together will,
in any event, depend on Europeans themselves.

Culturally speaking, Europe is a civil society. In recent decades,
however, this civil society has come to depend more and more on the
guardianship of the welfare state. This has diminished citizens' independence of action and the exercise of their freedom in ways that
make it difficult for Europeans, in both East and West, to meet the
expectations associated with a civil society.

The European experiment can succeed only if the citizens of
Europe manage to wean themselves of their dependence on a guardian
and interventionist state and develop a society in which they have
moved from a state-run to a civil society. The Member States and the
Union itself must support this process. Both levels, the individual state
and the European level, must expand the "area of freedom." The
Union especially must confine itself to the essential fields in which
one public authority can act for all, and at the same time, it must set
an example for the individual states.

We are still a long way from such an approach. By itself, the strong
emphasis placed on the principle of subsidiarity in the draft Constitu-

tion and in political declarations by the European Council will have no great effect. What must be done is to overcome the centralizing tendencies that have now gripped the EU, driven as they are by European and national bureaucracies. If the contradiction between the constitutional principle of subsidiarity and the reality of accelerating bureaucratic expansion with its centralist tendencies continues to grow, it will place in jeopardy not only the credibility of the Constitution, but also the inner cohesion of the European Union itself.

The question arises as to what extent the draft Constitutional Treaty is likely to help develop a European civil society, and thus to facilitate the development of the forces that will be decisive for Europe's inner cohesion. If we look at the Union's objectives from this point of view (Article 3 of the draft), we see that the first concrete objective mentioned is "the sustainable development of Europe based on balanced economic growth." The Union is to work for "a social market economy, highly competitive and aiming at full employment and social progress, and with a high level of protection and improvement of the quality of the environment. It shall promote scientific and technological advance. It shall combat social exclusion and discrimination, and shall promote social justice and protection, equality between women and men, solidarity between generations and protection of children's rights. It shall promote economic, social and territorial cohesion, and solidarity among Member States."

Turning to Part II, "The Charter of Fundamental Rights of the Union", it is striking that the fundamental rights are expressed very much in terms of the rights of working men and women, and of objectives for social security, especially in Title IV, "Solidarity." Even the legal, economic and social protections of the family are dealt with essentially in the context of working life.

Thus, large sections of the draft Constitution make clear that the European Union still sees itself primarily as an economic and social union. The draft here follows an approach that has been seen in recent years in resolutions of the European Council. This is especially true of the "special summit" in Lisbon in 2000. There, the way forward was described in terms of a new strategic goal that the Union set for itself "to become the most competitive and dynamic knowledge-based economy in the world, capable of sustainable economic growth with more and better jobs and greater social cohesion." This goal was to be achieved by means of an overall strategy "designed to enable the Union to regain the conditions for full employment, and to strengthen regional cohesion in the European Union." Growth targets were set that have since proved unrealistic, and full-employment objectives were formulated that ignored the reality of the labor market and the foreseeable trends.

Both the policy followed by the Union since Lisbon and the draft Constitution reflect the more general tendency to assume that the experiences of the industrial age and of industrial society are valid for all time. But even today these experiences are often no longer relevant. In the future they will lose even more of their significance. When the draft Constitution enters into force, therefore, a large proportion of its provisions will already have been overtaken by reality. This is true especially of the world of work. The Constitutional Treaty will protect not so much the working population as the acquired rights in which the outdated reality of the industrial society lives on. That cannot be the purpose of a European constitution.

The fact that the Constitutional Treaty does not go beyond the mainly economic character of European integration but, in effect, carries it forward in its objectives, and in other aspects as well, will prove to be one of the major problems facing the further political integration of the European Union. At bottom, the mistake that has thus far characterized the Member States and the process of European integration—the idea that the state can not only plan economic development, full employment and growth but can also use state resources to guarantee them—is being repeated in the draft Constitution.

The danger in such a policy is that it will necessarily lead to disappointment and will thus diminish the legitimacy the Union needs in order to be able to shape the future. I have been warning for many years, especially in light of the process of German integration, against expecting the motive forces for integration to come primarily from commitments to economic and social growth and prosperity. A European Union that, as its highest goals, promises full employment, gainful activity for 70% of the population of employable age, economic growth, increasing prosperity and comprehensive social security makes its existence dependent on its ability to achieve these objectives. If it cannot deliver, it does not simply lose a measure of authority and legitimacy: it endangers the inner cohesion of the Union and strengthens the tendency among Europeans to turn to their own states, with their supposed capacity to provide protection against the consequences of broken European promises.

If, therefore, we want European integration to last, we must ask ourselves in good time what will hold Europe together if economic and social promises cannot be kept, or cannot be kept in full. The question of what holds Europe together takes on even greater importance in times of economic and social tensions and crises. That such tensions and crises may arise in the coming years and decades is obvious. We must expect them. If in a united Europe we decide to give ourselves a constitution, we will do well not to fill it largely with economic and social commitments. It should rather set out the basis of an answer to the question as to what will hold Europe together even when economic and social promises fail to do so.

IV

For further political work in Europe, we need not only to identify other forces for political integration and cohesion, but also to draw conclusions for present and future European policy from the continuing fragility of that cohesion. Against this background, particular dangers for the inner cohesion of the European Union could arise out of the continuation of the policy of the welfare state, which, in major Member States such as Germany, France and Italy, has led to the virtually uncontrolled expansion of public debt and a steady increase in state intervention. Both of these developments cripple the economic forces at work and, as a consequence of the overextension of its responsibilities, weaken the state and its institutions. This provides special interests with a growing influence over the allocation of resources, thereby increasing the potential for conflict arising out of social policy.

This misguided development would receive special impetus from the enlargement of the European Union. The Union is being joined by ten states where social policy has been highly developed as a means of domination and where the capacity of large sections of the population to take responsibility for themselves is highly underdeveloped. A danger which I believe is just as significant is the possibility that European identity mediated through bureaucracy will obscure and neutralize the forces and values from which the unity of the Union and its legitimacy as the jointly defined community of all citizens in the Union ultimately derive.

Every bureaucracy—especially a European bureaucracy in alliance with the bureaucracies of its Member States—has an inherent tendency to shake off the substantive legitimation provided by the state and to become an end in itself, supposing itself to be the real supporting structure of the state's inner cohesion and purpose. This puts the bureaucracy in permanent conflict with the pre-constitutional forces, which in reality empower the entity that they have formed into a state and establish the goals towards which it is to work for the good of its citizens. Bureaucracies that step outside their service role cease to be servants and become masters, imposing anonymous control without transparent and personal accountability for the consequences of their actions. In the society in which they operate, they are not capable of generating inner cohesion resting on common convictions.

A solid European identity, a vigorous inner cohesion between Member States and citizens, can be ensured only if the incipient development of a European spirit of community is not overstrained but instead treated with care. This is true especially of the attempt to make the Union's inner cohesion a matter of the solidarity of the Member States and their citizens in European affairs. We should think twice before putting our trust in solidarity as a force for cohesion. First, there will be solidarity between the Union's Member States only insofar as their interests coincide. Divergences of interest between Member States can be overcome by calls for solidarity only to a limited extent.

In societies constitutionally formed into states, making solidarity effective by the enactment of laws (collective solidarity) presumes an inner cohesion in the community strong enough to allow the burdens associated with state-imposed solidarity to be absorbed. In other words, legally enforceable solidarity does not create inner cohesion; it assumes its existence. The European Union must therefore be cautious in making demands on its citizens in the name of European solidarity. In addition, it is one of the foundations of a civil society that it seeks a balance between personal and collective solidarity. A readiness for personal solidarity is as much an integral part of a society of citizens as is a readiness to assume responsible freedom. The advocates of state-organized solidarity who deny that readiness are denying the possibility of a civil society.

This brings us back to the acknowledgment of a principle that is also relevant to the process of European unification and to Europe's inner cohesion: the strongest bond within the Union is provided by common interests. The best way to shape the Union is to genuinely limit European institutions to European essentials and to renounce excessive regulation, overt or covert extension of responsibilities, the prevention of diversity in the name of the need for uniform regulation, and all forms of government guardianship.

The draft Constitution makes no great contribution to the realization of these insights. That is why it is not widely seen by the public as a genuine recasting of the European Community—in so far as the public is aware of it at all. A political debate on the new Constitutional Treaty in the European Union that is worthy of the name has yet to take place. Without such a debate we will not be able to deepen our understanding of the forces on which we will depend if Europe is to endure as a political union.

ERNST-WOLFGANG BÖCKENFÖRDE

Conditions for European Solidarity

I

To answer the question as to what are the conditions for European solidarity, we first need to clarify and understand what is meant by solidarity and what it involves.

a) In general, solidarity means first of all a certain attachment among people and reliance upon one another, because human beings cannot lead meaningful lives alone. That is the empirical aspect.

Related to this, solidarity signifies at the same time a form of assuming responsibility for one another, associated with positive action or services on behalf of others, whether individuals or a particular community or society as a whole. This is the normative aspect. Seen as such, solidarity goes beyond mere recognition of other persons as individuals in their own right, beyond the elementary injunction not to harm or interfere with others: it is concerned with community links and community-oriented activity. Seen in this way, solidarity is a generic, open concept. It gains specific content from the *nature* of its attachments and dependencies, or, more precisely, the nature of the social and community relationship wherein solidarity is desired and demanded of individuals. A commercial union requires solidarity on trade questions, but it does not require political solidarity.

The situation is similar with a sporting association or—European—sports union. Solidarity here is concerned with the needs and interests of the sport and nothing else. The crucial factor is thus the *telos*, or goal, of a community. It defines the specific content of the attachment as well as the mutual reliance, or empirical and normative solidarity. The solidarity required in a free trade zone or economic community is thus different from that demanded by a political community. Consequently, the meaning and demands of solidarity, what its conditions and requirements are, cannot be discussed in general, but only in concrete, terms.

b) If we turn our attention to the conditions for *European* solidarity, this presupposes an answer to the question of the *telos*, the purpose and goal, of European integration, specifically the European Union as enlarged by the ten new Member States admitted in 2004.

1. Within the EU, there is no clarity on this point. On the question as to the goal, or finality, of the European Union, there is currently a fairly diffuse collection of views, and the discussion, where it takes place at all, is remarkably fragmented. Several possible options and concepts can be discerned:[1] Europe as a framework for peace, with integration marking the final end of nationalistic conflict; Europe as a liberal market economy with free competition as the source of prosperity, and a functioning single market open to world trade as a goal in itself; Europe as an economic and social arena with the harmonization of living conditions as a form of inner-European redistribution and development policy, as well as with frontiers erected against the outside world to preserve the relative homogeneity of the Western European industrial nations; Europe as a powerful player in the global competition for technological and economic leadership, requiring a targeted industrial policy and concentration of forces in competition with the outside world; Europe as a great power based on its unified economic might, serving as a platform for action to exert its political will.

These concepts and options coincide and coexist, but to some extent they also conflict. Where their realization is concerned, a rather aimless pragmatism prevails, because the Member States do not pursue a common agenda but have different aims in mind.

The UK's objective for the EU is more that of a free trade zone and limited customs union, not at all a political union with, say, an autonomous external and security policy. This is deeply grounded in the UK's understanding of itself as a former world power and the primary ally of the USA. The new Eastern European members see the EU primarily in an economic development union, providing them with access to the economic freedom and welfare, along with the associated alignment and equalization effects. As for a political union entailing their own incorporation, their attitude, so shortly upon achieving their sovereignty through emancipation from the Eastern bloc, is more skeptical, seeing instead—as supported by experience—the USA as the guarantor of their security, not least of all vis-à-vis Russia.

The core European countries, the original states of the European Community, adhere more closely to the idea of a *political* union, through which—however internally organized—Europe can act as a political power and player, autonomously from, and in independent partnership with, the USA (and, shortly, Russia and China).

2. Given these differences, is a Europe of different speeds the appropriate solution? This may appear so, but caution seems indicated. For the problem at issue here is not having different speeds towards a common goal, but different goals for the unification of Europe. The outcome is not merely a matter of different velocities, but of two different Europes: a closer, politically unified Europe, and a looser Europe unified only in economic terms. These two Europes would then in turn need to be reconciled.

In what follows, I will seek to answer the question posed at the beginning by assuming as a working hypothesis that political union is the goal of European integration. What type of solidarity would be necessary to achieve this? What are the conditions and factors needed to bring it about?

II

For the European Union to emerge as a viable political union, it will need political solidarity (in both the empirical and normative senses). What is meant by such political solidarity in relation to the EU?

a) Generally speaking, political solidarity is not a form of solidarity confined to a limited sector of social life, such as the economy or sports, but one that embraces co-existence in its generic, overarching—that is to say political—dimension. In the EU, it involves living together in common with other peoples and nations in such a way that the community thus formed is, and remains, viable and able to act as a political community. To ensure the (normative) solidarity necessary for this purpose is a goal that is both accepted and acted upon. But it is not enough for all in such a community to be human beings and to acknowledge one another as such. What is also needed is a certain degree of common ground, a certain consensus on how people understand themselves and understand certain principles of living together in common.

This consensus emerges in questions such as "who are we?" and "how must we live together and how do we want to do this?" It may leave room for substantial differentiation, individuality and variation (and will need to do so), but must at the same time exhibit a rational and, to some extent, emotional common ground. This provides the basis for a shared "we" feeling to emerge and sustain itself. As an impartial Swiss observer puts it: "Between the elements to be integrated there must be links and connections, there have to be concordances, similarities and complementarities that have evolved over time. What is completely alien cannot be joined together."[2]

Such a shared "we" feeling, or identity if you like, entails that those things which affect the other also concern me, both intellectually and emotionally, and are not disconnected from my own existence. This provides— as a manifestation of solidarity—the basis for the recognition of shared responsibility, mutual support and cooperation. This is the "sense of belonging" mentioned by Lord Dahrendorf, the awareness and sense of community and the willingness to form this community, belong to it and participate in it—both in good times and in bad. One example: northern and southern Italians differ in many respects, and perhaps they are not very fond of one another. Nevertheless, what they have in common, as Italians belonging to the Italian nation, ultimately motivates the continuing transfer payments from the industrialized prosperous North to the poorer, less-developed South.

Only separatist movements that call into question this very unity can object to this. Political solidarity as discussed here needs to be more strongly present in a democratically organized community than in an authoritarian society. In the latter, the decisions taken to preserve order, resolve conflicts and reconcile interests have only to be accepted by the people as given. In a democracy, they have to be positively supported by the people as decisions emanating from and adopted by themselves. This is most clearly illustrated by the acceptance of majority decisions that are opposed to one's own views and interests. Adolf Arndt, the eminent social-democratic parliamentarian and jurist, formulated the problem succinctly: "democracy as a system of majority decision-making presupposes agreement on that which cannot be voted upon."[3]

b) But what are the conditions and factors for such political solidarity? What gives rise to such a common ground and attachment that is associated with and supports a political feeling of belonging together, expressed as "we"-consciousness and common identity?

1. Here, closer examination turns up a number of factors. Firstly, there is religion or confession—or several confessions of one religion alongside one another, provided these confessions adopt converging, rather than opposing, positions on the principles and forms of human co-existence. This provides the basis for far-reaching, deeply rooted shared responses to the question: who are we and how do we want to co-exist?

Then there is the question of belonging to a particular people. Here, some misunderstandings need to be countered. That which constitutes a people is determined only to a small extent by natural, or biological, factors, and much more by cultural factors such as language, customs and shared identity. What then makes a group of people such a 'people'? Werner von Simson, a committed European, commented as follows:[4] essentially, this group of persons sees themselves as a people and knows they are distinct from other groups in sharing memories and hopes, commonly experienced suffering and contempt, shared success and pride, and perhaps also a common myth or heroic image. Seen in this way, a people is characterised by a pre-rational collective consciousness and memory kept alive and preserved over generations, while nevertheless changing over time. This explains, on the one hand, the continuity and assimilative power of a people, along with its distinctness, but also, on the other hand, the potential for development and change in identity and individuality, so that a new, differently oriented and wider awareness can take hold.

Then there is—of special importance over the past two centuries—the matter of national awareness. National awareness refers to a common *political* self-awareness, associated with a desire for political independence. A nation and national awareness are not the same as a people and popular awareness, although they now often converge.

Crucial for national awareness is its political character, whereas for 'a people' an ethnic and cultural common ground and an identity based on it suffice.[5] A national awareness can exist independently of awareness as a people—the criteria for belonging to a nation are different and are determined by the nation itself as it forms. This is shown by the quite different nature of national awareness in, say, France, Germany and the USA.[6] National awareness can embrace different ethnic and cultural identities and preserve them as such—as shown by Switzerland, with its three to four ethnic and cultural identities within a united political confederation.

Finally, a further factor that should not be underestimated is a firmly established cultural heritage connected with a particular way of life or concept of order, accepted as a common basis for identity and preserved as such. The content of this common ground may vary and is not confined to a particular type. It may be characterized, say, by a conscious deference to diversity and plurality on the basis of the recognition of fundamental human rights. The result is a mentally internalized, conscious culture of tolerance as the commonly accepted form of living in community.

2. Of crucial importance for our context is that the various factors described here as mediating and supporting political solidarity coexist alongside one another. They are not mutually exclusive, but can instead complement one another and even be linked together, albeit not without tensions. History offers numerous examples, such as the link between the Catholic religion and national identity in Poland, the more distant co-existence between religion and national awareness in France, the tension between the national idea and the Islamic religion in modern Turkey and the overarching concept of the nation in the USA, incorporating a conscious culture of tolerance in connection with civil rights and the constitution.

This multiplicity of forces that bring about and support a necessary common ground means that, when one of these supporting forces declines or disappears, another can, to some extent, replace it. The relative common ground or homogeneity needed by a political community as the basis for, and expression of, political solidarity therefore does not depend on just one specific force or factor. These forces can in fact supplement or even alternate with one another. What is crucial is the outcome: the existence of a relative common ground supporting a political community, regardless of what it is based on.

The discussion so far has to some extent constituted a preliminary explanation, necessary for the central question that concerns us. We have now arrived at the crucial point: which factors or circumstances that give rise to the necessary political solidarity of the European Union are able, or needed, to support it? As such, which are essential if the aim of progressive integration is to be achieved?

c) Our point of reference here has to be the EU after its enlargement to the East, recently concluded and entering into force next year, i.e. a European Union with 25 Member States and peoples.

1. A common religion can be considered as a candidate to only a very limited extent. Although the peoples forming the EU adhere to the Christian religion, they generally do so only in a rather formal sense. Not only do the quite considerable differences between the Catholic, Anglican, Protestant (further divided into Lutheran and Reformed) and Greek-Orthodox confessions play a role, the crucial factor is that most of these peoples live in secularized, laicized societies in which religion is not just free, but also voluntary.

With freedom of religion generally recognized, it no longer constitutes the binding basis for shared co-existence, but merely one way of life which people may choose to adopt or not. However, the Christian religion, regardless of the differences between confessions, may be considered as a common cultural heritage that has molded and formed people over the centuries, with a corresponding effect on their thinking and attitudes. To this extent, while it can now no longer provide the basis for a European identity; it forms part of the shared cultural inheritance—based on the Greco-Roman, Judeo-Christian and Germanic traditions, along with the Reformation and Enlightenment—from which Europe draws sustenance.

2. However, in reality this common cultural inheritance turns out not to be a single generic entity, but a highly differentiated, diverse heritage. It has crystallized as numerous, nationally based, individual cultures, each forming separate ethnic and cultural entities, each with their own identity. In these, the peoples and the ethnic cultural religions of Europe, there is a sense of "belonging" that provides a basis for political solidarity. This, however, has yet to be formed with respect to Europe and the European Union as a whole, although it might be under certain circumstances.

3. Shared history, memories of common defeats, victories and heroic deeds as factors determining European identity still seem tentative. Although European history, objectively speaking, certainly exists, it does not live in the minds of people, and is not perceived as such. The history of Europe is perceived by the peoples of Europe essentially as mutual conflict, the struggle of peoples for emancipation and self-determination, not as something that binds them together. History is experienced and recalled as the history of one's own people and one's own nation. The perception and recollection of European history as a shared history of conflict and antagonism, but also one of shared achievements and mutual attachment, must first be instilled (through common history books and history teaching). This is an educational and cultural task, and, if successful, will bring about a corresponding mental attitude among the people of Europe.

One may of course ask whether the liberation of Western and Central Europe after 1945, and Eastern Europe after 1989, can be considered as a mentally shared, jointly binding moment. While this could be a shared and jointly binding recollection, what is this recollection oriented towards? What is the point of view? In Eastern Europe, as I understand it, it is different than in Western and Central Europe. For the peoples of Eastern Europe, their history of liberation is primarily oriented to the independence and sovereignty achieved through liberation from the Eastern bloc, which needs preserving, and not so much to a new form of incorporation into a politically organized Europe. The recent choice in Poland and the Czech Republic to opt for the USA and against the major European powers is significant: they consider the USA, not Europe, to be the guarantor power which has made their freedom possible and defends them against new imperial ambitions on the part of, say, Russia. Can anyone blame them?

4. Can Europe, as a "community of values," be a point of reference and integrating factor? This community of values already exists in broad outline, if considered to constitute the recognition and achievement of a free, democratic political order and way of life based on the rule of law and the recognition of human rights. Such common ground is important as a condition and basis for a potential political union of Europe, but does not yet in itself provide the political impetus towards such a union. A community of values in this sense can be achieved separately in each Member State, enshrined in their constitutions, and does not necessarily call for political union, and political solidarity, as the only way it can be achieved and preserved.

5. What about the nation of Europeans and a corresponding national awareness as a point of reference and integrating factor? Although it would still be premature to speak of a nation of Europeans, raising it as a possibility is nevertheless not utopian. The European Union currently comprises separate peoples and nations, but awareness of a European cultural and, to some extent, political identity may emerge. This is a process that can, and will, be driven and promoted by the abolition of frontiers, increasing economic interconnections, closer contacts, intellectual and cultural exchanges and communications, progressively expanding European civil rights and, finally, joint European institutions. Some progress is being made. However, this process has a future only if this developing awareness of a nation of Europeans is regarded not as an absorptive, but as an overarching, concept, a shared common ground and identity that does not replace the particularities and identities of existing peoples, but preserves them as autonomous components. A glance at Switzerland, where this outcome—albeit over a smaller territory—has been achieved, is again useful. The result would then not be a unitary concept of the "the people" of a democratic Europe, but a twofold concept, tending to a dual "sense of belonging."

6. Finally, a crucial factor for building political solidarity is the determined political will of all involved. If Europe as a political union of the European peoples is desired by these peoples to the extent that they want to be part of a framework structured and designed in this way, and live within it together, this could provide the basis for a corresponding attachment and readiness, as a matter of course, to support one another.

d) Following this critical analysis of the concrete conditions and points of reference for a European political solidarity, the question remains: what is to be done? How can the relevant factors be advanced, strengthened, perhaps even triggered in the first place, to ensure that European political solidarity can emerge and, where it does exist, be reinforced?

The point of departure should not be sought so much in a European community of values, a topic discussed with particular frequency by the politicians. As mentioned, such a community of values is important as a common basis and should be cherished as such, but it does not in itself provide the decisive impetus towards political solidarity. Priority should be given, first of all, to a shared view of history among the peoples of Europe, wherein national histories are perceived and recalled as a part and factor in the history of Europe, as a common ground; secondly, to the development and promotion of a European national awareness that does not absorb the national identities of the peoples, but embraces—and thus indirectly supports—them; finally, to establishing a voluntary and emotional commitment to the political goal of presenting a political union as a shared community, and acting toward this end.

But how can this be brought about and achieved? To conclude, some suggestions that require flushing out:

Bringing about and maintaining a common view of history is primarily a task for schools and education, which must include the history of Europe as a subject in its own right, incorporating national histories and using coordinated, agreed-upon texts. In addition, three European languages should be obligatory subjects in the higher school grades, with a view to ensuring communication throughout Europe and mutual understanding. Anyone who thinks that this is not much, and will not achieve much, should recall the words of Jean Monnet, the father of the Schumann plan, shortly before his death: "If I were to start all over again, I would begin with culture."

Encouraging and strengthening the national awareness of Europeans will need to take two factors into account. Firstly, this will also require schools and education. No one should forget the importance of schools in the formation of national awareness in France and Germany (alongside the military as the "school of the nation"). How else could it happen that Upper Bavarians and East Prussians, Swabians and Friesians regarded themselves as Germans despite all their differences, and felt they belonged to the German nation, and the Savoyards, the Bretons, the natives of Lorraine and the coastal fishing people of the Gironde felt part of the "Grande Nation"? Indeed, the school was the 'school of the nation'—why should it not be likewise for the nation of Europeans?

On the other hand, national awareness is also especially inspired and stimulated by the impact of political action, symbols and, not least of all, forms of citizen involvement that ensure that Europe and the European Union are no longer experienced as foreign or distant, but as something which belongs to people and to which people belong, a matter in which they have a say. Consider how much European awareness has been strengthened here by the recent (ironically intended) talk of "old Europe." Here there is an interaction: credible initiatives and challenges emerging from politics, political action and existing or developing political frameworks can themselves form or strengthen a common political awareness and also, step by step, an emotional sense of belonging and attachment to the European Union. This in turn provides a basis and platform for further action and development. The same applies to the political will to achieve such a political union of the peoples of Europe, which can likewise be reinforced and consolidated only through such interaction.

Much will depend on whether and to what extent the European Union is seen and experienced as bearing responsibility for the common good. As long as this function, as at present, is considered to reside virtually exclusively with the national state, a European political solidarity will not yet have emerged. This problem can be addressed if decision-making processes and forms of participation to this end are developed in the EU to involve the people and citizens of Europe. The democratic foundations of the Union must advance in step with integration, as stated by the German constitutional court.[7] Here are, in my view, crucial tasks for the European constitutional convention, more important than questions of a single or dual leadership, rules on the division of competences and the balancing act between Council, Commission and European Parliament. All these issues relate to the cooperation between governments within the European Union, but do not touch upon the foundations of the European Union within its citizens.

Notes

[1] A detailed list may be found in Rudolf G. Adam, "Wo ein Wille ist, gibt es viele Wege. Die Diskussion um die heutige Gestalt Europas muß konkreter werden," *Frankfurter Allgemeine Zeitung* No 283 of 5.12.1995, p. 17.

[2] René Rhinow, "Die Zukunft Europas im Spannungsfeld von Integration und Föderalismus," in Walter R. Schluep (ed.), *Recht, Staat und Politik am Ende des zweiten Jahrtausends. Festschrift für Arnold Koller,* Bern/Stuttgart/Wien, 1993, p. 778.

[3] Adolf Arndt, *Politische Schriften,* Berlin/Bonn-Bad Godesberg, 1976, p. 128.

[4] Werner von Simson, "Was heißt in einer europäischen Verfassung 'Das Volk?'," *Europarecht* 26 (1991), p. 3.

[5] Friedrich Heckmann, *Ethnische Minderheiten, Volk und Nation,* Stuttgart, 1991, pp. 46–51.

[6] Ernst-Wolfgang Böckenförde, "Die Nation—Identität in Differenz," in idem, *Staat, Nation, Europa,* Frankfurt/M., 2000, p. 34 (41ff.).

[7] BVerfGE 89,155 (186).

HEATHER GRABBE

What Hope for Solidarity in the Enlarged Union?

Introduction[1]

In enlarging to 25 member-states and beyond, the EU will change its nature. It will move from being a predominantly rich country club to a truly continental union. On what basis will this large community of states live together? Today, European countries are more alike than they have been for 200 years, with nearly all being democracies and market economies. But although the shared values of freedom, democracy and market economics are necessary conditions for harmonious co-existence in the EU, they are not sufficient. The Union needs solidarity as well.

But it is difficult for any community to feel a strong sense of solidarity if it increases rapidly in size. "Why should we pay to help all these newcomers?" is a common social reaction, whether the community in question is a small village or the larger part of a continent. If a community's membership is clearly defined, it is easier for the members to accept that they should help each other. But when the community is growing rapidly in ways that the members cannot fully control, their feeling of sharing a common cause begins to diminish. This change in sentiment is evident within the societies of individual European countries, particularly if they are experiencing—or fear—a rapid influx of new immigrants. In many countries over the past decade, claims that immigrants and asylum-seekers are unfairly taking welfare benefits have featured in election campaigns, especially at the local level.

This phenomenon is also evident at the EU level in response to the forthcoming enlargement. Can people feel a sense of solidarity with other EU citizens when they live as far apart as Oporto and

Lublin, or Thessaloniki and Narva? Many people in the existing 15 countries express resentment at the prospect of a rapid expansion of the community to include one-third more members, all considerably poorer than the old members. The existing recipients of funds from the EU's budget—whether they are French farmers or the poorest regions in Spain—understandably do not want to lose their transfers. The current recipients of the EU's structural funds have made frequent reference to the "statistical effect" of enlargement: no Spaniard will suddenly become richer owing to the enlargement, but overnight, many Spanish regions will become far wealthier relative to the EU average, because that average will be pulled down by the entry of poorer new members.

But the question of solidarity is not just about the EU's budget; it goes much further than that. Solidarity has been a sort of emotional glue for the EU over the past half-century. Even if member-states have often behaved in a self-interested fashion, they have also shared a general belief in the idea that there should be an '*ésprit communautaire*,' a sense that EU policies should serve the common good. This sense is also evident among the new member-states. However, a country's willingness to make sacrifices for the good of its neighbors could diminish as the community widens and economic competition increases. Already in the accession negotiations and the pre-negotiations for the next budget round, any sense of altruism was quickly disappearing.

The member-states' increasingly self-interested behavior in the past decade has been due to a variety of reasons. Germany was traditionally the 'paymaster' of the Union, financing the lion's share of EU projects. The German contribution to the EU budget is still more than a fifth of the total. However, since unification in 1990, Germany has found its public finances under unprecedented pressure, owing to the cost and economic impact of integrating the eastern *Länder*. These pressures have caused the 'Nettozahlerdebatte' to rise up the political agenda, with more and more Germans questioning their country's traditional role. The German public's willingness to pay the costs of solidarity with poorer parts of the Union has consequently diminished. Unlike in previous enlargements, it is unlikely to increase after the present one, as signaled by Germany's reluctance to provide any extra money from its own budget for new members at the end of the accession negotiations in December 2002.

The new members will also find themselves under unprecedented fiscal pressure upon accession.[2] Even before their actually joining the Union, opposition politicians and the domestic press in several countries are demanding that their governments get a better financial deal out of the EU. These days, any government, wherever in Europe, that claims to be acting in the '*ésprit communautaire*' is likely to be asked by an angry domestic press why it is not defending the national interest.

This contribution looks at how enlargement will affect three dimensions of solidarity in the EU. One is the political atmosphere, which will become sourer over the next few years owing to the difficult negotiations that will follow the 2004 accessions. The second dimension is economic diversity, which will increase as a result of poorer countries joining the Union. Finally, there are the social changes occurring across Europe, and their impact on notions of solidarity within individual member-states.

Changing political atmosphere

Inevitably, the overall political atmosphere in the EU affects any feeling of solidarity. The first few years after enlargement will be a turbulent period for European politics, one in which notions of solidarity are unlikely to flourish. The 10 newcomers will upset the balance of power between the existing 15 members, and the dominant mode of behavior is likely to be dogged defense of national interests.

After the warm words of welcome in May 2004, the battle will commence on the EU's most fiercely contested issues. The new members are joining just as the EU is finalizing its new constitution, and deciding the tricky questions of representation and the allocation of money. The 25 countries are already arguing fiercely about institutional reform in the Inter-governmental Conference that began on 4 October 2003. It is evident that Poland will be as feisty as Spain in defending its voting power and demanding greater representation in decision-making, both in the Council and the Commission. Within months of joining, the EU-25 will also start work on allocating the EU's central budget after the current settlement runs out in 2006.

These debates could quickly turn acrimonious. The old members will be trying to hang on to their acquired rights—Spain to its regional aid and Britain to its budget rebate, for example. Meanwhile, the Central and East European members will fight very hard for more budget funds. The new members want to make up for what they lost in the accession negotiations, in which the 15 old members used their greater muscle to retain more than 90 per cent of the funds for themselves.

Once inside, however, the newly-admitted 10 will have votes and veto powers. They will want to exercise their rights to the fullest, ensuring that they get better deals in future. At the same time, the old members will be trying to hang on to their long-standing privileges. This combination of defensiveness among old members and resentment among new ones will make for longer and bitterer arguments than before—and reduce any sense of solidarity between countries. These battles will also be hard-fought because their outcome will reverberate for many years to come. The budget settlement will dole out the spoils until 2013, and the new constitution will decide the voting power of each country in future negotiations.

Negotiations in the EU will also become more complex, because the ten new members are wildcards in the new game. The present 15 members know each other well. When beginning a new round of negotiations, each usually has a pretty good idea of their partners' positions, as well as of the strength of the opposition to their own stance. But the addition of two-thirds more players will alter the balance of forces. Where problems—such as reform of the Common Agricultural Policy—previously reached a stalemate, the new members may break the impasse by taking one side or another. On many issues, their governments have no position as yet, so one faction or another can attempt to court each.

The new members are also unlikely to form an 'eastern bloc,' by frequently voting together. They will have a common interest in focusing the EU's budget on policies for economic competitiveness, because most are much poorer than the original 15. But on the majority of questions each country will have to fight for itself, so that shifting coalitions of new and old will emerge, and change according to the issue on the table. The lack of long-standing partnerships like the old ones that characterised the original six members—particularly the Franco-German relationship and the Benelux grouping—will also have an impact on member-states' willingness to develop solidarity policies.

Increased economic diversity

Debates about solidarity have often been mostly about money, as they will be again after the 2004 accessions. Since 1989, income gaps in all European countries have widened. Despite economic growth in the aspiring member-states, there are still large inequalities of wealth within the current EU-15. EU GDP per capita now averages more than €20,500, but the Czech average is only €11,380, while Hungary's is €10,384 and Poland's €8,061. However, the richest Central Europeans have converged with the poorest EU countries: Slovenian per capita GDP has now overtaken that of Greece.

The range of economic performance and income across Central Europe is wide. The Czech Republic, Hungary, Poland, Slovakia and Slovenia enjoy GDPs per capita that is between one-third and two-thirds of the EU average, whereas the remaining countries are below one-third of the EU average. GDP per capita in Slovenia, the richest EU candidate, is over €15,000, while it stands at just one third this level in Bulgaria and Romania.

There are considerable inequalities between regions in Central Europe as well, so it is important to look beyond the national averages for income and employment. Regional unemployment rates vary enormously, and income levels in the regions around capital cities usually greatly exceed the national average. Rapidly growing cities such as Budapest, Prague and Warsaw are already ineligible for some of the EU's considerable regional aid funds. The average income in Prague, for example, is now 119 percent of the EU average.

The speed with which the economic disparities between new and old member-states narrow will depend on whether the applicants grow at a faster rate than the current EU members. The EBRD estimates that these countries could achieve long-term average annual growth rates of 4 to 7 per cent.[3] But to realize this potential requires both high investment and rapid productivity growth. The World Bank estimates that the front-runner candidates are 20 years away from attaining average EU incomes. And during that time, EU incomes will continue to grow, so that catching up will require much faster growth or significantly more time, possibly as much as 40 years.[4]

Given this outlook, the enlarged EU faces the prospect of having to deal with considerable disparities between income levels over a long period. New budget lines may have to be devised to mitigate the differences in income and employment between cities and regions in the enlarged EU, since inequality has social and political as well as economic consequences.

In principle, the EU's common policies are meant to address precisely this problem of disparities. The Community budget therefore provides aid to poor regions and farmers. However, more than half this budget is spent on agricultural subsidies that often go to richer farmers, and distort fair competition. This policy is no longer justified, but in the budget battles between the different member-states, the basic objectives of agricultural policy have receded from sight. Instead of a policy that fosters economic competitiveness, the EU has created a cover-up for social security to farmers. Many people in Europe find it difficult to understand why farmers should be singled out as the one social group to receive direct aid from Brussels. Why does taxpayer solidarity, they ask, extend to farmers but not to steelworkers, coalminers or small shop-owners?

The EU cannot put off major changes in its agricultural policy for much longer, not only because of enlargement, but also because of world trade negotiations and consumer opposition to industrialized farming. The next few years thus offer a valuable opportunity to rethink common agricultural policy, and to better achieve its aims and objectives in helping poor farmers and rural areas.

With income differentials growing after enlargement, Europeans will also have to rethink the objectives of structural and cohesion funds. Whom do we want to help? Some economists argue that only states with less than 70% of the EU's average GDP should receive structural funds. The UK Treasury has argued, for example, that richer EU countries should not receive regional aid from the EU budget at all, but rather fund them from national sources.[5] Poland would qualify in such a case. But regional disparities in some of the EU's new member-states will be vast, and unemployment rates will vary tremendously. In some regions of Poland—for example, Warsaw—

the average GDP is high, and it would be absurd to maintain that an investment in Warsaw is also an investment in the poorest regions in Europe. If the structural funds are an instrument for equalizing income levels, some regions in the new member-states ought to be excluded. Overall, the EU needs to focus its regional aid on the poorest regions of the enlarged Union, regardless of what country they lie in. That is the only way to ensure that policies designed to promote solidarity between Europeans are not primarily determined by intergovernmental horse-trading.

The new member-states will not gain full access to the EU budget for several years after accession, and it will be nearly a decade before they are fully eligible for the bulk of agricultural funds on the same basis as the EU-15 countries. This prospect raises the question of second-class membership for the candidates, but it may also cause the new member-states to demand a fundamental change in the next EU budget. That could present an opportunity for the enlarged EU to fundamentally rethink how it deals with economic inequalities and rural development. The recommendations of the Sapir report offer many useful points for that debate, particularly in matching up the objectives of the budget with the EU's aims for long-term competitiveness in the Lisbon agenda.

The only way that European countries can ensure their prosperity in the long run is if they work together to develop economies that can cope with international competition. Good economic policy is good social policy, and vice-versa. But the EU can help in this task by promoting better economic governance in the member-states—by benchmarking their progress in achieving economic reform, for example—and by making sure that the single market maintains a level playing field for all member-states.

What future for the European social model?

One of the most evident ways in which Europeans are different from Americans is in their attitude towards inequality, and particularly towards the role of the state in reducing economic inequality within societies. The new members generally share the preferences of the old ones in this respect, having generally experienced less inequality in incomes across society during the communist period. They too are seeking a balance between economic competitiveness and social cohesion.

Many Europeans fear that globalization and international capitalism will erode European societies, widening the gap between the 'haves' and 'have-nots.' Others argue that liberalization and increased competitiveness for the European economy are the only way that EU members can ensure their prosperity in the long run. Some people envy the US economy's dynamism, while others fear that the social problems associated with American-style capitalism might be transplanted to Europe.

One of the EU's greatest successes is the creation of a single market covering 15 countries and an economic output that rivals the United States in size. After enlargement, that market will grow to nearly half a billion consumers. One of the aims of removing barriers to the free movement of factors of production was to increase Europe's international competitiveness: the logic was that if European companies were forced to innovate and become more efficient, they could better cope with international competition. But although many Europeans are in favor of a market economy, they do not necessarily want a market society.

The EU's social policies are somewhat haphazard, because most social issues are dealt with at the level of national, regional and local governments. But the Union has been moving towards more comprehensive policies on issues like social exclusion and fighting discrimination, with mixed success. This is clearly a policy area that will need further development after the 2004 enlargement.

How much solidarity will European citizens feel in future? Social change and the EU

Independently of the EU's official agenda, both old and new member-states are already facing major challenges as their societies change. Many of the current EU's member-states contain significant immigrant populations. In Britain and the Netherlands, migrants have, for the most part, been integrated successfully; but even there, tensions remain, as race riots in the north of England in 2001 revealed. Moreover, immigration and citizenship issues have grown in significance within the political agenda in recent years, as populist right-wing parties have exploited them for political gain in France, Austria, Norway, Denmark and the Netherlands. In Germany, the question of whether 'guest workers' should be given German citizenship divided the political class in the late 1990s, and the search for a new immigration law was lengthy and difficult.

Europe is experiencing falling birth rates, so it will need substantial immigration in order to have enough young workers to support the economy and pay the pensions of the aging population. Similar processes are at work in the new member countries. Few realize it today, but Eastern Europe could soon turn into a region of net immigration. Today, trade unions in Germany and Austria fear that labor migration in the wake of enlargement will cost jobs in the current EU. In 5–8 years, these fears will be long gone as European countries (including the new members) are likely to be competing for skilled workers from elsewhere in the world.

European countries have dealt with their minority populations using very different policies—from integration to assimilation to discrimination. Populations are becoming still more mobile, as the fall of the Iron Curtain and the introduction of the Schengen area of passport-free travel have redrawn the map of free movement across Europe. Some borders have become easier to cross, while others have become barriers to entry. These changes raise the question of whether the enlarged EU will need a common approach to migration and asylum issues, so that would-be migrants will face the same criteria for gaining entry and employment in each European country.

Labor market issues are increasingly connected with social change: employers facing shortages of key skilled workers are calling for governments to grant more work-permits to people from outside Europe. But these workers often want to remain as permanent residents, and bring their families with them, creating new challenges to social cohesion. At the same time, immigration of younger workers may be essential, as the current population of most European countries is ageing and birth rates are falling. This flow of people into and around Europe is likely to cause long-term changes to the social fabric.

The question is how to benefit from the dynamism that cultural diversity and social change can bring to Europe, and to ensure that there is sufficient social solidarity, so that different groups (whether ethnic or economic) do not become alienated from one another. Recent years have shown how easy it is for the far right in many countries to exploit people's fear of change, difference and competition, and to blame immigrants and minorities for social problems. One of the EU's greatest achievements in the second half of the 20th century was to knit populations together across borders through economic integration in order to reduce tensions and eliminate the incentives for armed conflict. The major challenge of the 21st century could be to reduce tensions between different groups within national borders as well.

Enlargement, combined with demographic and social changes, also calls into question who is European—raising identity questions. Enlargement brings the EU new neighbors, countries that are poorer than the existing EU. People in Ukraine, Belarus and Russia regard themselves as European. But many EU citizens have little sense of solidarity with those neighbors who need help to achieve stability and greater prosperity. The danger is that a bigger Union might become a 'Fortress Europe' if the EU's border policies increase the isolation of the countries left outside without solidarity policies to help integrate them into the rest of Europe.

Conclusions

Solidarity refers to a sense of togetherness, as well as to the practice of helping one another. Without a sense of common purpose, people are unwilling to come to one another's aid. The wealthier European countries are not going to help the poorer ones simply out of idealism, but they must do so through a recognition that their self-interest is best served by pursuing common goals. The EU was created because the people living on this crowded continent have to work together and their destinies are intertwined. Solidarity is about recognizing that the world is a big and complex place, and Europe a rather small part of it.

This analysis leads to the following conclusions:

– In the negotiations for the EU's next budgetary period from 2007 onwards, the member-states—including the new members—should think more objectively about what future policies the enlarged EU will need. They should not focus on past precedents for spending, but instead establish a set of policy goals to address the new challenges of economic and social cohesion after enlargement.

– Solidarity is not a one-way street. The poorer EU member-states should not define solidarity in Europe as just "the rich helping the poor." They need to ask themselves instead what they can contribute as well, and that means developing the capacity to use EU aid sensibly. Ireland and Portugal have spent EU money wisely, and their economies have benefited, whereas Greece failed for years to use EU funds to modernize its economy. Eastern Europe should learn from those successes and failures to make good use of EU money.

– Demographic change in Europe is already taking place, and immigration will be needed to ensure that our economies can continue to grow. Europe's political leaders need to explain to their publics how immigration is in their own best interests. Equally, they need to establish common EU policies to ensure that there are legal routes of managed migration, to halt the growth in people trafficking and to ensure that immigrants who become residents are integrated into society rather than socially excluded.

– Solidarity begins at home. All European countries are trying to find the right balance between economic competitiveness and social cohesion. They are facing similar policy challenges in reforming pensions, welfare benefits and healthcare. These policies are best managed at the national level, rather than through the EU's institutions, but the Union can help countries to benefit from comparing their experiences and sharing the best practices.

In the 1950s, the integration of Western Europe was spurred on by the experience of the war and the communist threat. Today, war is a distant memory to most Europeans and there is no communist threat. The peoples of Europe need a different reason to pull together. That reason is our common destiny. During the Cold War, problems on one part of the continent could be isolated from the rest because border guards stopped people from moving, and economic contacts were limited by trade barriers and mutual suspicion. But now the frontiers are more open and the economies are more integrated. War, instability and poverty in one part of the continent have an effect on all the rest. The only way each country can ensure the security and prosperity of its citizens is to work with all its neighbors in a spirit of solidarity.

Notes

[1] Part of this paper is based on a joint article by the author and Henning Tewes which was published in *Gazeta Wyborcza* in June 2002.

[2] See Heather Grabbe, 'The Copenhagen deal for enlargement', CER Policy Brief, London, Centre for European Reform, www.cer.org.uk., 2002.

[3] EBRD, *Transition Report*, London, European Bank for Reconstruction and Development, 1999.

[4] *World Development Report*, Washington DC, World Bank, 1997.

[5] HM Treasury et al., *A Modern Regional Policy for the United Kingdom*, London, HMSO, 2003.

JANOS MATYAS KOVACS

Between Resentment and Indifference
Narratives of Solidarity in the Enlarging Union

Does anyone still believe in solidarity between the "two Europes"? One thing is for sure: even those who regard the concept of European solidarity as ambiguous, overused and occasionally harmful love to talk about it. I am afraid that I also belong to this group. My only excuse is that I do not preach solidarity, just listen to other persons' "preachings." As in the case of the previous enlargements of the European Union, solidarity also features as a crucial component of a regular *rite de passage* today, when eight (plus two) ex-communist countries are being admitted to one of the strongholds of what they used to glorify or demonize as "the West." Ideally, this rite would require a cold-hearted, impartial analysis. As an Eastern European citizen, however, I cannot promise to properly meet that requirement. As a participant in the forthcoming admission (an anthropologist would say, initiation), I am unable to disregard the intrinsic ambiguity of the feast.

This paper revolves around the rival interpretations of "true" solidarity with each other proposed by the two halves of Europe. In what follows, I will make a distinction between two dominant discourses conceived of as ideal types: a romantic ("Eastern") and a pragmatic ("Western") one, based on altruistic and utilitarian considerations respectively. The incredible bipolarity of the real types of these discourses, which is also well known from the proverbial *Ossi–Wessi* conflict in Germany,[1] allows me, I believe, to commit all possible crimes against science one can commit in such a brief essay. My paper will be an orgy of oversimplification. I will use a primitive, two-actor model, in which the aggregate terms "East" and

"West" represent a large variety of agents and a great number of countries: Brussels and the EU member states; the members, the new entrants, the candidates and the "left-outs," the elites and the people at large, governments and oppositions, politics, business and academia, and so on, and so forth. Apologies in advance.[2]

In addition, solidarity will only be examined in a transnational framework, that is, I venture to explore a territory in which one cannot easily apply techniques that have been developed to understand, for instance, income redistribution at a national level, cohesion of social groups, or the exchange of favors within a family.[3] Fortunately, my task is not to assess the two actors' actual record of solidarity, but "only" to capture the underlying differences in interpreting the concept.

A surprise

Under communism, solidarity was a subject of black humor rather than of scholarship. An altruistic interpretation of transnational solidarity could not be accepted under the conditions of "forced solidarity," to use a euphemism for dictatorship and military occupation. Merely the name of the *Comecon* (Council for Mutual Economic Assistance) or the Soviet slogan "*druzhba narodov*" provided sufficient food for sarcastic thought. Let me quote my favorite joke on "mutual assistance" and "socialist brotherhood": "On a military training field a Russian and a Hungarian soldier find a bar of chocolate. They are terribly hungry. The Russian says solemnly: let us share it in a brotherly manner. God forbid, answers the Hungarian, we should split it up fifty-fifty." The message was clear: if solidarity is nothing but a farce, equal sharing becomes *the* just alternative. In Eastern Europe one did not have to nuance that proposition until the birth of *Solidarnosc*.[4]

Why deny it, the *ouvrierist* strand of anti-communism emerging in Poland at the end of the 1970s was a powerful challenge to me, a Hungarian economist who had left market socialism for liberal capitalism, and who did not want to stop along the way at a rather corporatist version of social market economy. *Solidarnosc* reached back to the world of ideas of the workers' movements in the 19th century, no matter whether Marxist, anarchist or Christian–Socialist, and put the emphasis on protecting/emancipating the weaker part, actually the majority, of society. Sporadic contacts between Eastern European dissidents aside, the notion of solidarity gained a transnational meaning and a justified fame in the course of the 1989 revolutions, especially in terms of helping the East German refugees and Romanian rebels. The internal cohesion of Polish anti-communism and the sweeping victory that irradiated to the former Eastern Bloc as a whole forced me to think twice before placing, in a sad gesture, solidarity à la *Soliadarnosc* under the heading of social romanticism.

Yet, the attraction of "unforced solidarity" evaporated with surprising speed (somewhen between the first quarrels within *Solidarnosc*, the political disempowerment of the Eastern lands in Germany, and the outbreak of the Yugoslav war) in our region, and I resumed my customary suspicion toward allegedly altruistic transnational relations, regardless of their origin. To my mind, terms such as *Realpolitik*, geostrategy, superpower interests, etc. outcompeted any notion of Europe-wide or transatlantic fraternity, no matter whether it came to Visegrad, the Pentagonale or NATO. To be sure, that suspicion did not lead me to equate, with an anti-imperialist zeal, the violence of Soviet-style "proletarian internationalism" with the peaceful (and largely understandable) asymmetry of the European integration project.

My personal story is irrelevant, but it explains the surprise I would like to share with the reader in this paper. In studying the current history of ideas in Eastern Europe, I could not help recognizing the renaissance of the concept of solidarity, in particular, in the context of EU enlargement.[5] My surprise stems less from that revival itself than from the crystallization of two rival discourses of solidarity on the two sides of the former Iron Curtain, which—unfortunately—reinforce each other, as in a dialogue of the deaf, without resulting in mutual understanding.

To quote a current example, in the course of running an eight country research project on cultural encounters in the economy between the East and the West, I am astonished daily by the extent to which the narratives of our respondents in our program's three target groups, Easterners and Westerners alike, are permeated by their views of European solidarity, no matter whether they are entrepreneurs, civil servants or academics. The micro-narratives allude to two macrodiscourses, both dealing with the East–West distribution of costs and benefits, with a special emphasis on the turbulent game of the Enlargement. I call them *"rhetoric of resentment"* and *"rhetoric of indifference."* (I leave the reader to guess which discourse comes from which side of the former Yalta divide.)[6] Although the two rhetorics conflict sharply as far as their arguments and style are concerned, their representatives are fairly interchangeable. Today it is extremely difficult to determine, both in the East and the West, whether a given narrative of solidarity with the "Other" has been produced by a soft populist, a pragmatic conservative or socialist, or a frustrated liberal.[7]

Undoubtedly, in the Eastern half of the continent, meditating on the East–West exchange of goods and cultures is an eternal pastime, in both its Westernizing and its nativist/populist versions, not to mention the plurality of their combinations.[8] In the course of admitting the former Eastern neighbors into the EU, however, no self-aware West European citizen can any longer afford to keep a low profile as to the balance of mutual transactions, either material or spiritual. The accession talks dealt with precisely such transactions; certain of the West's interests have fallen victim to the admissions, and, in principle, the newcomers have the right to renegotiate the balance at any future moment. In the West, the dominant event of the Enlargement has given rise to a dominant discourse, a partially new one, which pertains to that balance—in other words, to solidarity between the old and the brand-new member states.[9] Finally, there exists a Western discourse that eventually may go beyond "Orientalism,"[10] an attitude of condescension that is packaged, in the most favorable instance, in moderately polite phrases concerning the cultural traditions, revolutionary virtues, etc. of Eastern Europe.

How did the dialogue between the representatives of the two rhetorics begin? Let me avoid struggling with the conventional chicken-and-egg problem. Westerners contend that the dialogue began with Eastern complaints and passionate allegations, the Easterners maintain that it began with unfulfilled Western promises. Surely it went on, either with the deep silence of the West, which might equally reflect a bad conscience, indignation and indifference, or—increasingly—with an enumeration of the mutual advantages of the integration, and an introduction to the "manual" of social engineering in transnational communities. In contrast to the "invitee," the "inviter," the stronger party in the game, could more frequently afford the elegance of a less heated rhetoric.[11] Nonetheless, scattered references to the overambitious demands of the Easterners, as well as to their poor performance, bad habits, etc., remained an indispensable component of even the friendliest Western narratives.

While the two discourses of solidarity failed to meet, the bargaining over the Enlargement between the members and the would-be entrants continued. The asymmetric position of the two parties suggested that the rhetoric of resentment was invented to soften the pain of unilateral imposition, and to obtain a few exceptions to the admission rules. Similarly, the rhetoric of indifference seemed to serve as a simple cover discourse to justify why the West could not make more concessions in the bargaining game. My hypothesis is more benevolent than those interpretations. Beyond the ideologies required by daily politicking, I presume to find, in the divergent narratives of solidarity, deep-seated convictions reinforced by rational motives. By this I mean motives that are firmly grounded in past experience and do not aim at manipulation or self-deception. As with most rites of passage, large differences of interpretation between these convictions occur at the two ends of the passage. The fact that the diverging interpretations do not lack imagination and use a great variety of symbols, and, what's more, rest on rival concepts of rationality, must not lead the observer to take pleasure in detecting conspiracy and mass psychosis among the participants of this continent-wide dialogue.

In what follows, I will touch on four major issues:

– The semantic roots of the divergent approaches to solidarity.
– The difficulties in defining and measuring solidarity.
– The composition of the two rhetorics of solidarity.
– The chances for a rapprochement between the two.

Between two vocabularies

Suspecting a dialogue of the deaf, one is advised to reach for dictionaries. In looking up the word "solidarity" in English language dictionaries, I found the following definitions:[12]

– unity or agreement, especially among individuals with a common interest, sympathies or aspirations

- *mutual dependence*
- *mutual support or cohesiveness within a group*
- *complete or exact coincidence of interests*
- *an entire union or consolidation of interests and responsibilities*
- *fellowship*
- *community*
- *combination or agreement of individuals, as of a group*
- *complete unity, as of opinion, purpose, interest, feeling*
- *agreement between and support for the members of a group, especially a political group.*

In the English language, apparently, solidarity is not necessarily imbued with the altruistic value of *fraternité* and philanthropy. The emphasis is put on common interest, mutual dependence, and agreement (and the ensuing *esprit de corps*), rather than support. The words "solidary" and "solidaristic" hardly exist in English. If this meaning is badly needed, one may use the French original *"solidaire."*

To confess my ignorance, I have, until recently, replaced the word "solidarity" in English with a group of terms beginning with "co": companionship, cohesion, compassion, consensus. This bias comes from my mother tongue, Hungarian, or, in a wider context, from Central and Eastern European traditions as a whole. In Hungarian one cannot be solidaristic with someone out of self-interest, not even on the basis of a sober assessment of "mutual dependence" and reciprocity, or with an aim of "consolidating interests and responsibilities." If you strike a business deal or you forge a political agreement, this can reflect mutual dependence and rest on mutual concessions. Solidarity is, however, essentially unselfish, it pertains to assisting the weaker, with a bit of sacrifice at least, a sacrifice that is without material reward. What you gain from supporting others is—at most— purely moral gratification. Also, my fellow citizens would add, you cannot be solidaristic with the stronger or the more powerful.

When it comes to differences in meaning between Anglo-American and Hungarian terms of the same Latin/French origin, one had better consult a dictionary of German language. Small wonder that terms such as "support", "sacrifice", "fraternity" and "charity" (*Nächstenliebe*) are stressed there. In *Wahrig* or *Duden*, for instance, one comes across synonyms like *"gemeinsam," "einig"* and *"fest verbunden"* but, at the same time, they also focus on the *Solidaritätsprinzip* in Catholic social teaching (the theory of *Solidarismus*), which expresses the *"wechselseitige Füreinander-Eintretens (einer für alle, alle für einen)"* and legitimizes *"soziale Ausgleichsprozesse."* Furthermore, they make a sharp distinction between *"Interessenssolidarität"* (see, e.g., *Solidarhaftung* and *Solidarschuldner* in business law) and *"Gemeinschaftssolidarität."*[13]

I expected to examine a communication gap, and actually fell into a cultural abyss. The hope for mutual understanding between the East and the West, I thought, depends on whether or not the dominant discourse in the West can reasonably combine the Anglo-American (liberal) and the German as well as other European (social-liberal or conservative) readings of solidarity. However, things turned out to be much more complicated, and not only because one can easily get lost in the jungle of communitarian, egalitarian-liberal, multicultural, etc. theories.

Measuring solidarity?

I spare the reader most of the intricacies of measuring solidarity between two parties who disagree on the merit of the concept. Even in the best case, where European integration is a positive-sum game, opinions will differ on whether one can call a win-win situation a quintessential embodiment of solidarity. The typical answer by a Westerner would be the following: this favorable situation results from joining forces on the basis of our common interests and shared values, therefore we are definitely *solidaire* with each other. Synergy *is* a primary prerequisite to solidarity but redistribution (i.e., a sacrifice on our part) and leveling are not. If someone insists on the concept of support, no one will prevent him/her from using the word, because in the given case the stronger party actually helps the weaker one by means of cooperating on the basis of mutual advantages.

The Easterner, however, would argue in the following way: a win-win situation can only reflect solidarity if the weaker party gains (perhaps significantly) more in relative terms than the stronger as a result of co-operation *and* redistribution. This may eventually lead to a catching up with the West. If we, however, catch up without redistribution, there is no point to talk about "genuine" solidarity. In the opposite case, i.e. if the East gains comparatively less in the win-win framework, the Westerner will still continue to talk about solidarity, whereas the Easterner will begin to wonder why the West does not offer the East part of its own gains in order to reduce the distance between them. Why should one regard a widening of the gap between the rich and poor, the developed and developing, as a sign of solidarity? he/she will ask. According to his/her view, it is the entrants in this case who are, in a perverse manner, *solidaire* with the—stronger— member states, even if no direct redistribution takes place.

Questions upon questions, though we have not yet considered the problem of absolute gains and the games without "happy ending," i.e. the win-lose and the lose-lose situations. For instance, continuing to presume rather optimistically that the win-win thesis[14] applies, the two sides may nonetheless disagree on the preferred size of the sacrifice. The Easterner can be modest (or diplomatic) to ask only a small sacrifice of the West in relative terms, because he/she is aware of the fact that, given the vast differences in the status quo, small sacrifice in absolute terms is equivalent to a large support in relative terms in the East, and will result in a fairly high pace of catching up.

Conversely, he/she can challenge the West by fixing an arbitrarily chosen, quick pace of leveling as a *conditio sine qua non* of solidarity, and by deriving from this pace claims for the absolute size of support. On its part, the West can choose from a large repertoire of responses, ranging from the dry message of "be happy that you aren't losing" to what I would call "realistic generosity." By the latter I mean the implementation of the elastic idea of "give the East as much as necessary to prevent it (and the enlarging EU) from declining, and as much as possible in terms of the stability of the West." The elasticity of the idea becomes transparent in particular when win(East)–lose(West) and lose-lose situations appear on the horizon of integration.

In any event, what notion of gain is to be applied? As with all theories of distributive justice, the devil is in the details of defining what exactly is being distributed, and in what manner. Is it income or wealth, or opportunities for generating them? Is it a material or a spiritual good? What is the time frame of distribution? One party may lose in the short run, only to win in the long run. Winning might also mean that you lose less than you would have lost if you had not taken part in the game.

The game of integration consists of numerous subgames. Are the gains in these subgames really measurable by the two actors *and* commensurable between them? How do we calculate, for example, the decline in the sovereignty of the entrants, and how do we compare the result of our calculation with the growth of agricultural subsidies allotted to them? I am afraid that measuring is a no less perplexing task if one studies the pluses and minuses in the same field, say, sovereignty. Can we reasonably compare sovereignty losses that are due to the imposition of the *acquis communautaire* in the candidate countries with sovereignty gains that are due to new freedoms granted by the same *acquis*?

Let us suppose the impossible: that all short- and long-term gains and losses of the Enlargement are quantifiable (or at least predictable) in both halves of the European economy. We know not only all price indices, trade figures and employment indicators, but also the monetary equivalent of each and every indirect effect of economic change on air pollution, life expectancy, or propensity for migration. Moreover, the balance of all genuinely political and socio-cultural transactions between the East and the West is precisely drawn. Let us also presume that, at the end of the day, the entrants will be net recipients of the integration in all respects of the overall give-and-take. Yet, even in this Paradise we will certainly hear many Easterners lament: "the concept of solidarity must not be expropriated even by a far-sighted and all-encompassing but exclusively technical calculation. You, Westerners are not quite solidaristic with us if you write us a thousand billion euro cheque but deliberately drop it to force us to bow down before you." It seems that there is no path that leads out of the cultural abyss.

Rhetoric of resentment

The Western reader may find the metaphor of the cheque pathetic,[15] the feeling of humiliation exaggerated, and the damage caused by what the Easterners consider impolite behavior reparable. "Sooner or later, the synergetic effects of the integration will convince them of their hypersensitivity, as happened in the case of Spain, Portugal, or, more recently, East Germany," he/she would contend optimistically. Evidently, the growing "accession fatigue"[16] among large segments of societies within the new member states today, and the disillusionment with the record of solidarity coming from the West, would be less widespread if the citizens of Eastern Europe were sure that the above-mentioned cheque had actually been written. At this point, however, they feel increasingly reassured to the contrary: no generous cheque has arrived yet in Budapest, Prague or Warsaw, which may well mean it will not arrive later, either.

Today, it is relatively easy to make pessimistic long-term predictions such as these (let me stress again, without a special populist bias) in the region:

- Given the less favorable starting conditions, the success stories of previous enlargement rounds cannot be repeated.
- The entrants will stay in the poorhouse of the Union, torn out from their natural (Eastern European) environment. The best of the former outsiders will become (and remain) the worst situated insiders.
- The EU regulations (administered by the Brussels bureaucracy) will slow down economic growth, invalidate the entrepreneurial skills of the new Eastern capitalists, and dismantle economic and social regimes of high efficiency, which have emerged after communism under global/American influence.
- No one will guarantee our catching-up with the EU average and compensate for its future costs. At any rate, the relative backwardness of East Germany demonstrates that an ex-communist country cannot hope for leveling during a single generation's lifetime, even if a generous cheque continues to arrive each year.

This paper is not about the cost-and-benefit ratio of the Enlargement. Similarly, it does not want to decide whether or not the popular mind is wrong in feeling a sense of humiliation and showing a propensity for depressing scenarios in the future. Are these traits due to the well-known paranoia of small nations in Eastern Europe that instinctively distrust any "new hegemony"? Are they rooted in their secular inability to make a distinction between better and worse hegemonies? Do they try to overcompensate for their inferiority feelings and/or the fact of being exposed to a thorough examination by the West? Are the communists, the nationalists, the conservatives, or any combination of them, responsible for making the public attuned to the nightmare of neo-imperialism? Be it as it may, there already exists a detailed *Leidensgeschichte* of the Accession; a story that is ritually told in the region. Let's begin our brief hermeneutic expedition by reconstructing this "tale of woe."

The lamentations about the alleged misdeeds of the West begin with the "original sin" of rejecting, in 1989, the project of European reunification, and replacing it with the foggy prospect of gradual integration.[17] The Grand Illusion of inventing, in a joint effort, *the* good society was thereby replaced by the everyday boredom of seeking compromise between various bureaucracies.[18] In fact, membership in the EU was not conceived of by the West as a quasi-natural entitlement a country merits because of its geographical position, or as a moral compensation for suffering under communism. To a large extent, the Easterners still remember their own tribulations as a service rendered to the West. The context was granted by history many centuries ago: accordingly, Eastern Europe (especially its Western borderlands) constitutes a buffer zone between civilization (Christianity) and barbarism, the inhabitants of which do their best to arrest Oriental invasion.

Evidently, an immediate reunification in 1989 would have been regarded by the citizens of Eastern Europe as a courageous and magnificent act of solidarity on the part of the "lucky half" of Europe. They made repeated attempts to convince the West of the fact that this act would demand less sacrifice than a gradual solution. They referred to the danger of communist restoration, to the economic and political destabilization of the buffer zone, and, in a self-ironical tone, even to the risks of forcing the "bad children" to play in the yard. "We make a bigger noise outside than inside, under strict surveillance", they said, "and tomorrow we will bring in more mud on our shoes than today." "Please mind," they went on, "that if you make us wait too long in the cold then you will have to face exhausted and angry youngsters in the new family." No success whatsoever…

To be sure, sharing the luck in order to help the unlucky catch up was not only a sentimental desire by the Easterners, but also a strong gesture made by quite a few politicians and prominent intellectuals in the West during the Cold War. Since then, the theory of "having been left in the lurch by the West" (a historical component of any rhetoric of resentment in Eastern Europe) could always find a sympathetic ear in the region. All the more so as, right after its "defection" in 1989, the West returned to (more exactly, remained in) the ex-communist countries, assuming the combined roles of business partner (investor, privatizer, economic advisor, etc.), political ally of the future member states of NATO and the EU, and—rhetorically—cultural companion of the old European nations in the East. These nations had, by the historical accident of Sovietization, remained separated for half a century.

"You deserve to return to Europe, you are one among us," the West communicated to the East, "but please wait a little, first we must adjust to one another." Initially, the core of the Western discourse in its various roles did not differ much in its passionate emphasis on mutual adaptation and solidarity, no matter whether the latter concerned job creation, teaching business culture, assisting democratization, providing military defense, or supporting spiritual renewal.

While in business *strictu senso,* no sensible Eastern European citizen could trust in good faith in altruism,[19] the verbal gestures of inclusion on the basis of historical/cultural proximity *did* raise bold expectations in the would-be European countries. At the beginning of the 1990s, one might have believed throughout the region that the indisputably large gains obtained by the West from the first moments of post-communist transformation would pave the way for a fast and rather smooth political enfranchisement of a large part of the former Eastern Bloc by the Union. Yes, one could expect that EU members would be in solidarity with the potential entrants at least in a *narrow sense* of the word: the West would take the political and socio-cultural risks once the economic risks were abundantly covered by profits earned, without making special efforts, in the emerging markets of Eastern Europe and by way of a reduction in military spending.

"Not only our past suffering but also our current revolutions have directly contributed to your welfare," the Easterners told the Westerners. "We do not beg you to do us any favors, and we might also relieve you from your historical debts. But please do not forget about your most recent windfall profits." In this way, the West was not asked to compensate for its gains during the era of *Ostpolitik* and *détente*,[20] and the East also seemed ready to cancel the moral debt originating in the West's indirect responsibility for the consecutive tragedies (1956, 1968, 1981) of the "other Europe." A new—European or Euro-Atlantic—Marshall Plan was, however, mentioned as an appropriate device with which to cushion rapid admission to the Union.[21]

It came as an embarrassment for the applicants that, in West European attitudes towards the Eastern neighbors, the principles of natural entitlement and cultural proximity were not maintained or, in the worst case, were replaced by that of co-option based on general reciprocity. The latter would imply the above-mentioned exchange of risks *without* examining the performance of, or making distinctions between, the newcomers. The principle of overall reciprocity promised virtually the same outcome; i.e. admission by "birth" or by—largely indirect—merits achieved earlier throughout the region. By contrast, the EU did not suspend the rules applied in previous enlargement rounds, and insisted on the principles of individual (direct, non-historical) merits and competition among the accession candidates. It thus applied a procedure that was defined by entrance examinations, performance criteria, hurdles, roadmaps, etc., which resulted in dividing the countries into groups arranged vertically on a long waiting list.

Admission to a club, athletic game, school enrollment, parental help, job interview, guided tour, military training, etc.—even if the West has not always employed exactly these metaphors, the East translated the incoming paternalistic messages with their help, and slowly gave up its own optimistic metaphors ranging from love, marriage and a friendly reunion to the exhausted sailor who finds refuge in the harbor after the storm, to the more pragmatic image of risk-sharing in a non-profit insurance association. These metaphors were chosen to reflect symmetric relationships, fast mutual acceptance, and trust, all based on moral virtues, traditions and an exchange of favors, rather than on a certain level of performance at a given moment.

Yet another blow to Eastern European self-esteem occurred when it became clear what the EU meant by "preparedness to join," what kind of performance counted, and how it was measured. Here the tale of woe rose to epic heights and became filled with a whole series of concrete offenses that the region allegedly had to endure in the course of the Enlargement. Indignation was caused by both the philosophy of screening and its implementation, not to speak of its language:

"The European Commission focuses on legal performance rather than on the socio-economic culture of the candidates;" "the criteria of selection between the would-be entrants are inconsistent"; "the rules of the game reflect the worst of what social engineering can produce, including the fact that they undergo changes in the course of the game"; "the liabilities of the East are overestimated while its assets are undervalued, and the price it has to pay for the integration is ignored by the West"; "the alignment with the *acquis* excludes the takeover of other than a diluted model of European capitalism"; "the selection procedure is distorted by *ad hoc* (geo)political decisions, financial constraints, etc."; "the Enlargement is controlled by incompetent officials who waste time as if they had been commissioned to delay the accession"[22]; "competition incites the candidates against one another"; "the end result was pre-programmed by a centuries-old symbolic geography, i.e., a traditional bias of the West toward East-Central Europe"; "the expected level of preparedness is higher than it was in the case of 'Southern Enlargement,' while the support provided by the Union is much lower"; "no one spoke about Eastern Enlargement when Austria joined the EU"; "accession is a heavily hierarchical term"; "two-track/speed Europe, *Kerneuropa*,[23] etc. serve as linguistic means of exclusion of the Eastern periphery."

One could list the complaints, which culminate in accusing the West of Orientalism or—in a more radical fashion—of imperialism,[24] without end.

Beyond a certain point, the West had practically no chance to evoke sympathy for its strategy of enlargement, as all its moves were interpreted within a framework of resentment. The *Leidensgeschichte* ended with peculiar conspiracy theories (I use the populist terminology to sharpen my point): "The *compradores* sold our nations to the new invaders for peanuts"; "the Westerners need us (our land, our talent, our moral standards, etc.) much more than we need them"; "the *acquis* was invented to paralyze competition coming from the East"; "what happens is actually a Westward enlargement[25] of our unique values, which has been marketed by the West cunningly as Eastern

Enlargement"; "in sum, we are enriching the West, which is a sheer nonsense"; "as with the Soviets, solidarity is just a codeword for exploitation and unequal exchange."[26]

Solidarity is a fragile commodity. One has the impression that, in deciding whether or not the West showed solidarity toward the newcomers, the latter were influenced at least as much by the choreography (scenery, language, symbols, images) of the accession as by the size of the transfer payments, or the entrants' voting rights in the enlarged Union. They felt provoked by the coldly critical remarks in the country reports, by the Brussels delegation's rigorous claims and reserved style, by the secretive world of administration in the Commission, by the constant postponement of the accession date, and by the incessant repetition of the civilizing messages ("wait a bit and clean up your house," "put your things in order," "adjust to the European level," "develop, discipline yourself, leave your bad habits behind," etc.).

These messages were imbued with a warning: "don't forget please that *you* are the ones who want to join *us*." Symptomatically, this sentence was interpreted by the East in the following way: "they in the EU say that they are doing us a favor by accepting our application." This interpretation anticipated the Eastern attitudes toward the Accession Treaty. The "take it or leave it" principle applied by the West at the end of the accession talks (and sugarcoated only by minor concessions) was regarded by the entrants as blackmail. "Why does the West not at least pretend that it respects us?" they asked angrily.

Sheer populism? Even liberals in Eastern Europe could share this anger with some reason. Certain aspects of their reservations (cf. overregulation, legalism, social engineering, Europe vs. America, etc.) have already been mentioned. An additional ground for anxiety, however, distinguished them from the Western Euroskeptics: the asymmetry between Brussels and the new entrants mobilized the worst attitudes that had been developed way back under communism in the hearts and minds of the latter.

Thus, quite a few "bad habits" of the Easterners have been reinforced, rather than eroded, during recent years. For instance, what we called "plan bargaining" ("performance hoarding," "rule bending," etc.) in the command economy—implying a complicated double speak (and double-dealing) with the authorities, and a constant fishing for soft regulations and exceptions to the rules—was revived in the framework of the accession talks. Similarly, intrigue between the candidates behind each others' backs and striving to forge a special relationship with Big Brother also reminded the observer of the "good old days" of the Soviet empire.

Cumulative frustrations notwithstanding, the rhétoric of resentment is more than merely a sentimental or, on the contrary, a sneaky variation on the themes of historical debt, moral responsibility and the like. Its language is partly rational, wherein rationality goes beyond the minimum level required for inventing a game strategy. This rhetoric includes a peculiar mix of requests and charges. It can be sarcastic, bitter, even furious; nonetheless, it rests on a specific concept of solidarity.

A close reading of the East's dominant discourse reveals that, apart from the obvious attempt at gaining as much support from the West as possible in the shortest period of time, the entrants put forward quite a few rational ideas of distributive justice. Indeed, they did their best to maximize the balance of transfers, prolong the advantageous derogations, and shorten the life of the disadvantageous ones, etc. They were aware of the size of support the EU member states (former accession countries) had received thus far, and used these figures as benchmarks of fair treatment, dignity, etc., in the accession talks.

Rational reasoning did not end here. As we have seen, the newcomers did not refrain from comparing costs and benefits ("we give more than we take"), suggesting risk sharing ("we have made substantial payments in advance"), or calculating opportunity costs ("the Enlargement will be more expensive if you delay it") when they tried, by means of utilitarian arguments, to persuade the EU of the need for showing more solidarity. Among these arguments, however, two plausible suggestions were missing: to my knowledge, no serious program has been recommended by the East to introduce a sort of "solidarity tax" (following the German example of *Soli*) and/or a "solidarity loan" in the West.

The new member states want to catch up quickly. This is the cornerstone of the moral economy of the East, but does not aim at instant leveling by claiming a large part of the wealth (income, welfare) of the older members. At the same time, the Easterners are not willing to tolerate alms. They do not wish for the West to lose when the East gains, but they cannot imagine solidarity without real sacrifice on the part of the stronger party. If both parties win, then, in their opinion, the relative gains must differ in favor of the East in order to secure medium- or long-term leveling. Provided that this higher percentage does not come about autonomously, the West is asked to channel part of its gains to the East.

This is a necessary condition of solidarity. The entrants are convinced they are not asking too much. Donating, say, one per cent of Western GDP to the East could replace (or trigger) a several-percent growth in our half of the continent, they observe wistfully. Maybe it is just a "first push" that is lacking, the argument goes, and redistribution could come to a halt fairly soon thereafter, since the relative gains will be higher in the East.

Why are even such rational messages misunderstood, misinterpreted or simply disregarded in the West? Are they inextricably mixed with historical/moral arguments? Are they just poorly elaborated? Do they rest on a concept of solidarity to which the addressee cannot subscribe? Or is the West plainly disinterested in listening to the messenger?

Rhetoric of indifference

One cannot help, in asking these questions, witnessing the deep-rooted indifference that the West has betrayed in responding to (or triggering off) the rhetoric of resentment. I hasten to add that I do not mean by indifference either a lack of a moral(izing) approach to European integration, or a low profile of tactical moves in the accession game, or a total repression of negative sentiments. On the contrary, the member states did not reject the ethical conclusions of the entrants' solidarity narrative as a whole (supporting the weaker members of the "family" is, namely, part and parcel of the foundation ethos/myth of the Union). Rather, they frequently used the image of indifference to improve the bargaining position of the West in the course of the Enlargement, and they could not conceal some of their Orientalist prejudices toward the newcomers.[27]

Indifference reflects three things: *a)* a principled disinterest in an overwhelmingly altruistic approach to solidarity, in historical arguments on reciprocity, and in vague ideas on distributive justice and social engineering; *b)* an instinctive inattention, originating perhaps in aversion and fear, toward any kind of reasoning based on the concept of the victim and his/her *ressentiments* and toward any "culture of complaint"; *c)* a calm attitude of the "seller" toward the "buyer" in the sellers' market of the accession.

Consequently, the West did not think it had to make special efforts to challenge the main tenets of the East's discourse. The entrants still experience this neglect as humiliating (and mistake it for condescension, or even hatred), which in turn drives their resentment even further, thereby widening the communication gap.

As a rule, the representatives of the rhetoric of indifference limited themselves to pragmatic/utilitarian arguments. Interestingly enough, they did not present the final objective of the East's catching up as questionable. Instead, they kept silent about the distant future, and focused their criticisms on another *leitmotiv* of Eastern narratives of solidarity, namely, the claim of redistribution. The main aspect of this critique came as a surprise: "Why does the East not realize that direct support may wrongly serve the end of leveling? Does it wish to jeopardize its own project?"

The Easterners responded indignantly. They did not understand why they could not build consensus around their own concept of solidarity with the Union that also loves to advertise categories such as identity, belonging, the family of nations, cultural/religious traditions, citizenship, social cohesion, the European Social Model, etc.[28] By a reflex motion, the Easterners associated these categories with forgiveness, biased rules, altruism, moral responsibility, permissiveness, the exchange of favors, and generosity, applying the *Solidaritätsprinzip* of "one for all, all for one."

It took some time for the East to recognize that the West went beyond the biblical analogy of the prodigal son:[29] its paternalism was not humble and unconditional, fueled by affection and bordering on self-punishment. The *pater* called the European Union decided to be strict and demanding, rather than generously tolerant, and if it nonetheless made an exception to the rule, this stemmed from his own interest, rather than from a personal bias toward his son. Nothing should invalidate the underlying maxim of initiation: "first prove that you are able to live with us under the same roof," wherein equal emphasis was placed on "prove," "first" and "able." This rite of passage also stipulated the right of the father to specify the initial conditions of cohabitation, e.g., the way in which decisions were made in the family, or the kind of assistance the son received from the close relatives.

In what follows, I will arrange the main elements of the rhetoric of indifference according to the six principal tropes of its Eastern counterpart.

Accession as a quasi-natural entitlement

Geography and history, of course, matter. However, they are only necessary, but not sufficient and not at all well-defined, conditions for claiming support from the West. Solidarity has not only an East–West axis, but also a North–South one, with far larger masses of "deserving poor" in the developing world. A large part of these (e.g., people in the Mediterranean region) can also prove their geographical and cultural proximity to Western Europe.[30]

Furthermore, as the example of Turkey or Israel (or, for that matter, that of Russia) shows, the cultural geography of Europe is too shaky to sustain an operational theory of solidarity. Because symbolic boundaries (religion, arts and sciences, social doctrines, etc.) are fuzzy, the EU has to insist on practical considerations in order to avoid endless cogitation over questions like "is Romania more European than Croatia?"

Along with the alignment with the *acquis* and the Copenhagen criteria, a crucial consideration is the general workability of the Union. The capacity of the EU for altruism is limited, according to the West, actually much more limited than that of the Western parts of Germany, and the poorer member states, as well as the poorer regions or groups of citizens in the member states, also compete for help. They, too, are "naturally entitled." The larger the number of "natural" claimants, the lower the probability of finding viable patterns of cohabitation, and the higher the probability of organizational overstrech.

Moral responsibility for Eastern Europe

This is again a fairly inoperational concept, especially in a transnational context. It competes with the principle of national and Union-level responsibility. "Until we have our nation-states," the Westerner admits, "we will probably feel more responsible for the destiny of our lower-middle class than for that of other countries' underclasses."

Even in the case of Germany, in which the principle of the nation was not expected to constitute a huge obstacle, moral responsibility for the former GDR has remained a fiercely contested concept. Moreover, like the notion of natural entitlement, the term of responsibility may imply admission to and/or support from the EU, but it does not specify the terms of admission and guarantee the pace of catching up with the Union's average (why not with its most advanced members?) by the entrants. "In any event, what could explain a moral choice that prefers the victims of communism to those living in our own former colonies?" the Westerner asks.

Paying historical debts

"Is there anyone out there," he/she will continue, "who could calculate our bills from the past? What is the starting date of the period of calculation: The stopping of the Mongol invasion? The ousting of the Turks? The Paris peace treaty? Munich? Yalta? Why not forcing the Russians to pay? We did not colonize Eastern Europe, why should *we* compensate its citizens today for what they lost under communism? True, the West was relatively lucky but who says one has to do penance for its fortune?

Anyway, we also sacrificed part of our welfare in the arms race while contributing to welfare under communism and/or to the implosion of the Soviet empire. Don't panic, we will pay because we do feel *some* responsibility for you (in particular, once you are in the Union), but please avoid this perplexing talk of historical debts. Or— *ad absurdum*—tell us how much the well-supported East Germans owe to the poor Russians today, and don't forget about drawing a balance between what Hitler did to the Russians and Stalin to the Germans. Wouldn't it be more useful for both of us to draw a line and break with the practice of looking backward? By the way, could

you please tell us how *you* treat your Eastern neighbors (or the citizens of the Eastern part of your own country)? Have *you* already
paid all your historical debts?"

Reciprocity and risk sharing between East and West today

"In principle," goes the argument, "this scheme of solidarity would
be acceptable for us if the 'favors' granted by the East were not overestimated, while the services rendered in return were not systemati-
cally undervalued. First of all, the accession countries have profited
tremendously from the inflow of Western capital thus far; this was the
only way in which they could avoid total collapse. Similarly, if admission to the EU had not materialized, they would have risked the same
outcome. Secondly, by that very inclusion, the West offers the East not
only new market opportunities, employment possibilities, and transfer payments, but a variety of other benefits ranging from a security
umbrella for investors through growing monetary stability, business
networks and education, to the brand name 'Europe.'"

The entrants can continue freeriding on a much larger scale. And
these are merely the economic advantages; advantages that could not
have emerged without some sacrifice on the part of the member
states. The same applies to political and socio-cultural opportunities:
the "community achievements" being assumed by the East with much
complaint reflect a large array of hard work, conflict, self-restraint—
in a single word, *sacrifice*—made at earlier stages. Leaving the East
in the lurch? A false accusation!

From this perspective, inclusion itself is tantamount to solidarity
based on support and sacrifice, especially if one considers the risks
of allowing the East to use Western societal regimes. The accession
may imply yet further sacrifice if the entrants abuse those regimes by
way of tax evasion, corruption or ethnic strife, all favorite topics of
Western populism, which unfortunately signal real dangers.

"Thirdly," the Westerner continues, "much of the risks are even
less predictable than these. By experimenting with deepening and
enlargement simultaneously, and by co-opting an unprecedentedly
large number of relatively backward countries, we took a bold step
that, in retrospect, may well turn our former sacrifices into futile efforts.
Extrapolation is in vain. But how to share risks without knowing their

dimensions? Perhaps if we were able to calculate the balance of costs and benefits properly (including political and socio-cultural ones), it would not be the West, but the East, who should pay. In such a case, why should we spend more than absolutely necessary for damage control on the East?"

Instant/quick accession as a proof of solidarity

"You accuse us," says the Westerner, "of committing the 'original sin' of missing the historical chance for instant European reunification. Are you aware of the complexity of such a vast social engineering project? Careful preparation, thorough screening, institution building on a large scale, legal and cultural adaptation, etc. take a long time. It was also out of solidarity that we wished to spare the East the shocks typical of the across-the-board unification process in Germany. Haste may result in a situation in which both parties would be worse off in the near future. Please also be mindful of the fact that some of the earlier EU candidates had to wait longer than you for membership. We cannot simply renounce our entire philosophy of piecemeal social engineering, which has been corroborated by the centuries-long experience of making democratic capitalism work and coping with inequality in Europe, and, more recently, by the construction of the European Union."

In an ideal case, this philosophy includes the following principles:

a) The EU takes an organic/evolutionary approach to institution building, which includes long-term regulations, stable and formalized rules, a cautious combination of societies with divergent pasts, a gradual leveling of old and new members, etc. It would be an unjust simplification to call this a bureaucratic stalemate.

b) The workability of the integrated system is a main priority, and because it is contingent on the abilities of the individual members, prudent selection and preparation of the candidates are indispensable tasks. Transfers alone, however large they may be, do not create viable institutions. And, conversely, faced with the lack of appropriate institutions/cultures, even the most tight-fisted support cannot be absorbed, or it will leak away due to ignorance, neglect and corruption.

c) The EU prefers steady and homogeneous systems of regulation with only a few unavoidable exceptions, and no double standards. Any divergence from the established rules of accession, for instance, would be unfair to the participants of the former enlargement rounds, and would provoke resistance. Because the Union fears corruption, accession deals based on an exchange of favors, informal bargaining, obscure transactions, etc. are to be ruled out *ab ovo*. "We do not grant special favors," says the West, "we just establish the hurdles. Anyone who can overcome them, has the right to join (upon being invited, of course)."

d) In order to avoid conflicts of interests, the candidates are not allowed to take part in deciding on the terms of their own admission to the Union. This is, of course, asymmetry by definition, but only of a temporary kind. By and large, democracy begins after the accession. As a matter of fact, no one compelled any of the entrants to apply for admission.

e) Consensus-building,[31] shared values, common identity, European citizenship, etc. are important pillars of cohesion/solidarity within the Union. They should rest, however, on a negotiated coordination of particular interests. Romantic promises will not help.

f) The organization potential for social engineering in the EU is restricted, and budgets are under severe constraints. Thus, common tasks must be prioritized. Eastern enlargement, for example, had to wait for the completion of previous accession projects, and was delayed by the deepening as well.

g) Although the Union is keen on reducing inequality between member states, it cannot guarantee the pace of catching up for the above reasons, as well as because of the self-imposed limits to redistribution between the member states.[32]

h) The historical bills presented by the East compete with future payments demanded from the West. In endangering internal solidarity within the member states by indulging in nostalgia, the entrants may paralyze the future of the entire continent within the global competition. Engineering requires a constructive attitude, and the suppression of dissatisfaction with the allegedly unfair distribution practices of the past, in order to ensure distributive justice in the future.

i) The EU does not live in a vacuum, free from the concerns of *Realpolitik* (including geopolitics). The proportions of size and power between member states are not disregarded in decision-making. No matter whether we like it or not, there *is* a core and a periphery in European integration.[33] The interests of the member states are more important than those of the future entrants. Additionally, the Union's political and socio-cultural goals cannot persistently counteract the objectives of economic integration. The members cannot have their cake and eat it. The given stage of the business cycle is a crucial variable of Union-level policies. Those who happen to enter the EU during stagnation or recession are victims of bad luck.[34]

In sum, accession is not a panacea. If launched too early and badly managed, it can spoil the chances of the East's being supported, not to speak of the implementation of its final goal of catching up.

Distributive justice and catching up

The principles of fair distribution within the Union are defined less strictly than those of social engineering. The maxims "there is no free lunch," "merits first, rewards later," "no help without self-help," "the assistance should be transparent," "charity is just an auxiliary solution," "the donor has the right to check the recipient," etc. are the familiar rules of thumb of textbook capitalism. These maxims were widely used during the accession talks to urge the East to leave its postures of "learned helplessness" and "subsidy addiction" behind. In so doing, the West proudly presented its stronger ego, i.e. the meritocratic (versus the charitable) one during the pedagogic exercise.[35]

"We have been socialized in a culture of self-reliance," said the Westerner. "If we really left our Eastern neighbors in the lurch, then it would be high time for them to follow the example of Baron Münchhausen, and pull themselves out of the morass by grabbing at their own hair. Charity disguised as solidarity would demobilize the entrants and impair their ability to catch up. Empowerment is a better solution; offering the East a single fishing net rather than tons of fish promises a more robust procedure of catching up. Subsidies would only give birth to new subsidies; support is a Pandora's box. At any rate, how can one vehemently make a claim for assistance and complain about the loss of sovereignty at the same time?"

Hence, redistribution from the West to the East should be scrupulously apportioned. But what will be the end result of just redistribution? Catching up has many faces. Should it result in an equality of opportunity or outcome? Should the entrants target the representative middle of the member states, or the most advanced among them? Whom among the would-be entrants should the West support: those who perform better or worse? Do those who give more also deserve more? "It would be stimulating to meditate upon these issues," says the West. "Unfortunately, our opportunities are severely limited; solidarity as support can only be sold to our electorates if it does not jeopardize the status quo. Anyway, why should even the Western underclass eventually support the Eastern upper class?"

Chances for a rapprochement

It is not my intention to situate myself in the middle ground between these two discourses, and assume the role of wise and neutral arbitrator. Yet, I could do so, because the rhetorical conflict conceals a great variety of overlapping ideas and discursive techniques, even if the stylised arguments reconstructed above suggest an extremely deep cleavage between them. That is why I have tried to call the reader's attention to quite a few pragmatic considerations within the rhetoric of resentment, and to a fair degree of resentment within the rhetoric of indifference. Why cannot these commonalities nonetheless bridge the communication gap between East and West?

I am afraid that the conflict between the two discourses of solidarity is, by definition, irresolvable. The dialogue is fruitless not only because of the divergent value orientations and semantic approaches, and the strong link between the rhetoric and the actual strategies of bargaining over the accession, but also because both discourses rest on a number of assumptions that can only be checked (if at all) many decades from now. Hypotheses such as the one that postulates catching up without generous redistribution cannot be proven by reference to previous EU enlargements, which were much more open-handed toward Greece, Portugal or Ireland than the current one is to the ex-communist entrants.

Conversely, it would be difficult to verify the assumption that rapid accession accelerates leveling between old and new member states, because precedents are lacking. In making a case for their own rhetoric, both parties rely on the only available real-time experiment, the process of German reunification. Unfortunately, both discourses find enough evidence in that experiment to validate their own messages.

If the reunification of Germany is regarded as a successful story of catching up (because the average rate of leveling has been high during the past fifteen years), the Westerner would say: "Look what an exorbitant level of support is needed to offset the adverse effects of instant accession!" The Easterner would respond in the following manner: "Now you can see that it is only a combination of quick accession and generous redistribution that can fill secular gaps in development."

If, however, the German experiment is thus far considered as a partial failure (because leveling slowed down considerably during the past decade), the Westerner can assert: "Look, even such an exorbitant level of support is insufficient to redress the balance impaired by instant accession!" And the Eastern reply would be: "Because even a combination of quick accession and generous redistribution does not guarantee a sustainable pace of leveling between the Eastern and Western lands of Germany, imagine how slow our catching up will be if you insist on 'realistic generosity,' that is, if you remain so selfish."

Of course, these reactions can be nuanced, but it is likely that the indignant questions "why aren't you more generous?" and "why aren't you more grateful?" will recur in the dialogue of the deaf. Similarly, recriminations such as "you are just moralizing to raise funds" and "you just talk about gradualism since you do not want to help us now" will not fade away. Moreover, day-to-day bargaining will unavoidably reveal double standards in the strategies of the two parties from time to time, a fact usually not conducive to mutual trust.

Today, with a lack of powerful common enemies,[36] the forces driving reconciliation are feeble, and the two halves of Europe are not compelled to rethink their own interpretations of solidarity. Hence, given the West's favorable bargaining position, for the time being I can only imagine a kind of "unilateral rapprochement," to use an oxymoron, between the two rhetorics. In other words, this will involve a unilateral adjustment by the East, or—loyal to the well-known traditions of Westernization in Eastern Europe—a simulated one.

Meanwhile, provided the enlargement is successful, the entrants may actually reconcile themselves to a less romantic concept of solidarity. Instinctively, they will strive to reduce cognitive dissonance, and view the EU as a good choice. Once they enter the West, they will be confronted with less humiliation because the enlargement will operate as a self-fulfilling prophecy within the Union: "We admitted them to the club," the Westerners will argue, "*therefore* they can't be too bad."

This prediction may moderate the Orientalist prejudices. Departing from an outright rejection of the enlargement, a radical populist in the West can arrive at a reserved statement such as "once those over there join the West, they probably cannot remain Easterners for good." In this more relaxed atmosphere, the new members will be tempted by an interest-based approach to solidarity, as has been suggested by the West. In fact, they have already been so tempted. In response to the growing resentment of their Eastern neighbors, in particular those who have not yet been invited even into the Union's waiting room, a familiar attitude is becoming more and more fashionable among both new members and current entrants. I would describe it as "indifference."

Katzenjammer

This paper has grown out of a conference presentation made just before the official admission of the first eight ex-communist countries to the European Union. It bore the title, "On the Eve of a Gloomy Feast." Although it was clear to most observers at the time that the feast would be a bit sad, I promised to celebrate it as an unprecedented act of European reunification. Falling in love with my own concept, I put my faith in the inertia of the attitude of indifference. In other words, I assumed that *a)* the West would be protected against the adverse effects of the Enlargement for a sufficiently long period; *b)* the European Constitution could be endorsed (even if by a small margin) by the national referenda in the core countries of the EU, and the latent conflicts between them would not burst out soon; *c)* the debate about the accession of Turkey would—fortunately—steal the show from the one concerned with Eastern Enlargement. Hence, a large part of Eastern Europe would "creep into" the Union under the aegis of a "normal" amount of indifference. Thus, the images of the proverbial Polish plumber and the Hungarian truck driver could not be exploited to spread *réssentiment* amidst domestic and intra-EU political quarrels in Western Europe.

True, clouds began to gather around the next budget round before the feast began, but I did not expect the state of indifference to be disturbed from within the "old" Union, resulting in a falling degree of redistribution in favor of the new member states. As a consequence, instead of witnessing a gradual reduction of resentment in the East, one sees additional arguments emerging in the region to support the old belief of "having been left alone."

"We accepted the limitation of labor migration to the West, but no one told us that the Bolkestein directive granting the freedom of movement for service providers would not come into force, and our legal migrants should face popular distrust, hostile trade unions and harassment by the police." "We thought we would have the right to decide about income and profit taxes in our countries, and that no Western politician such as Nicolas Sarkozy would threaten us with reducing transfer payments if we went on with what he calls 'tax dumping.'" "We expected to remain under close surveillance by Brussels, but did not know that we had joined a community in which influential leaders such as Jacques Chirac could instruct us to 'shut up.'" "How does the Union dare to demand solidaristic behavior from us, while it descends into petty bargaining over less than a half percent of the EU's aggregate GNP?" These stylized sentences are meant to reflect the present mood of political, business and cultural elites in the new and future member states.

Theoretically, these elites could have a unique chance, I believe, to alter their traditional roles for a moment by contrasting the growing resentment in the West with cool-headed, pragmatic reasoning (bordering on indifference) about balancing interests, assuring the viability of common institutions and the like. What we have instead is a wide stream of the usual complaints, suspicions, renewed talk about dignity, and, last but not least, a romantic gesture of self-sacrifice by the Eastern European prime ministers at the Brussels summit in June of 2005. In a heroic (pathetic) move, they demonstrated the readiness of the "New Europe" to cut its own funding in order to save the Union's budget.

"When I heard one after the other, all the new member countries, each poorer than the other, say that in the interest of reaching an agreement they would be ready to renounce some of their financial demands, I was ashamed," said then-EU President, Jean-Claude Juncker. Apparently, he took this gesture of solidarity at face value. Most other leaders of Western Europe were said to suspect calculated behavior behind the newcomers' pedagogical ambitions.

Welcome back to square one in the game called transnational solidarity in Europe...

Notes

[1] For the limits of the explanatory power of the analogy, see the penultimate section of the paper.

[2] Probably, I would not dare to afford this luxury if I were a specialist of the economic and political history of European integration. Thus far, I have made only two and a half attempts to interpret the current round of EU Enlargement, and even these were excursions to intellectual rather than "real" history. See J. M. Kovacs, "Westerweiterung? Zur Metamorphose des Traums von Mitteleuropa," *Transit* 2001/21; "Approaching the EU And Reaching the US? Transforming Welfare Regimes in East-Central Europe: Rival Narratives," *West European Politics* April 2002; "Rival Temptations—Passive Resistance. Cultural Globalization in Hungary," in: Peter Berger & Samuel Huntington (eds.), *Many Globalizations*, Oxford University Press, 2002; "Little America," *Transit* 2004/27.

[3] For an early approach to moral principles in the international political economy of income redistribution, see Amartya Sen, *Resources, Values and Development*, Oxford, 1985. See also his *Inequality Reexamined*, Oxford, 1992. The economic branch of postcolonial studies also revolves around the problem of distributive justice in North-South relations. Today, one can observe an upsurge in the institutional theory of foreign relations. See e.g., M. G. Cowles et al (eds.) *Europeanization and Domestic Change*, Cornell UP, Ithaca, 2001; A. Stone Sweet et al. (eds.), *The Institutionalization of Europe*, Oxford UP, 2001; E. O. Eriksen, "Towards a Logic of Justification. On the Possibility of Post-National Solidarity," in: M. Egeberg and P. Laegreid, (eds.), *Organizing Political Institutions*, Oslo, Scandinavian UP, 1999; F. Schimmelfennig, "The Community Trap. Liberal Norms, Rhetorical Action and the Eastern Enlargement of the European Union," *International Organization*, 2001/1; U. Sedelmeier, "Eastern Enlargement: Risk, Rationality and Role Compliance," In: M. G. Cowles and M. Smith (eds.), *The State of the European Union: Risk, Reform, Resistance, and Revival*, Oxford UP, 2000.

[4] An important exception to the rule was a promising but rapidly aborting debate in the middle of the 1980s about unequal exchange in the Comecon. According to an iconoclastic view in Soviet studies at the time, the Soviet Union was "exploited" by the satellite states in its trade with them in the

so-called "socialist world market." See M. Marrese and S. Richter (eds.), *The Challenge of Simultaneous Economic Relations with East and West*, New York UP, 1990; J. Brada, *Interpreting the Soviet Subsidization of Eastern Europe*, MIT Press, 1988.

5 The IWM projects "After the Accession... The Socio-Economic Culture of Eastern Europe in the Enlarging Union: An Asset or a Liability?" and "Dioscuri. Eastern Enlargement—Western Enlargement. Cultural Encounters in the European Economy and Society after the Accession" embrace eight countries of Eastern Europe (Bulgaria, Croatia, the Czech Republic, Hungary, Poland, Romania, Serbia/Montenegro and Slovenia). To a large extent, the following arguments are based on many dozen in-depth interviews and private conversations that I made during the past five years with leading participants of the accession game in both politics and business as well as in the academia in the framework of the project, and also on a preliminary analysis of hundreds of interviews and dozens of case studies, media- and literature reviews completed by my colleagues in the eight countries.

6 In what follows, I will use the term "rhetoric" more often than that of "discourse" in order to point to the persuasive thrust of the given narratives.

7 This convergence, of course, makes my life of an analyst easier but why conceal the fact that I am not that happy witnessing the dire state of liberal thought in the West and the dilution of the Westernization paradigm of the liberals in my own region. The example of "Euro-realism" propounded by Václav Klaus in the Czech Republic shows much in common with the attitude of "entering Europe with national pride" by Viktor Orbán in Hungary.

8 See J. M. Kovacs, "Uncertain Ghosts. Populists and Urbans in Postcommunist Hungary," in: Peter Berger (ed.), *Limits of Social Cohesion*, Westview Press, 1998.

9 This discourse on solidarity is not without antecedents. Besides the relationship between the EU and the developing world, it builds on the ongoing debate between the Union's net payers and net recipients in general, and between the developed and less developed regions of Europe (e.g., North vs. South Italy, West vs. East Germany) in particular.

10 Cf. Larry Wolff, *Inventing Eastern Europe*, Stanford, 1994; Maria Todorova, *Imagining the Balkans*, Oxford UP, 1997; Iver Neumann, *Uses of the Other*, Minnesota UP, 1999.

11 In the West the production of vicious figurative slogans is left to the Haiders, Bossis and Blochers. However, I am afraid that even they cannot beat the Csurkas, Leppers, Sheshels and Zhirinovskys in hate speech.

12 I applied a random selection from various editions of Oxford, Cambridge and Webster dictionaries, and made only minor simplifications in the texts.

13 I do not want to bore the reader with the nuances of the term "solidarity" in other languages. For still influential definitions, see Piotr Kropotkin's "natural solidarity" (a natural law describing spontaneous compassion rather than rational choice) and Emile Durkheim's distinction between "mechanical" and "organic" solidarity.

14 For the Easterners' propensity to expect lose-win situations to emerge, see Georgi Ganev, "Economic Attitudes after Ten Years of Transition," in:

Political and Economic Orientations of the Bulgarians, Centre for Liberal Strategies, Sofia, 2000.

[15] Some years ago, in Eastern Europe the press was still full of the "we cannot trade money for pride"-style declarations, and of the frustration felt over the lack of an elegant—even if symbolic—gift given by the West to the East at the end of the accession negotiations with the "first rounders." Instead, the region received the infamous Rasmussen documentary on "The Road to Europe" that revealed a deep condescension felt by the Danish prime minister especially toward Poland. Disillusionment is also reflected by a new genre of Eastern European witticism, the EU jokes. Let me quote three of them: "Why is the EU like a cemetery? Because we will all end up there." "Why do we enter the EU? Because we have not been invited to join the US." "Why does the EU enlarge itself to the East? Because there is the Ocean on its Western border."

[16] A feeling of popular discomfort was demonstrated by the accession referenda, especially in Hungary and Slovakia (as regards the voters' turn-out), and Latvia and Lithuania (as regards the proportion of the yes votes).

[17] The most offended were the former dissidents who, after a while, put the Western attitudes under the heading of "usual geopolitical practices" that ranged from Yalta, through 1956 and 1968, to 1981. For a recent recollection of this view, see e.g., Bronislaw Geremek, "Welche Werte für Europa?" *Transit* 2004/26; Ulrike Ackermann (ed.), *Versuchung Europa. Stimmen aus dem Europäischen Forum*. Frankfurt a.M. 2003 (humanities-online.de).

[18] Cf. Tony Judt, *A Grand Illusion? An Essay on Europe*, Hill and Wang, 1996.

[19] In 1989 still quite a few economists in the region put their faith in a comprehensive debt relief.

[20] "Do not panic, our cheap revolutions will be followed by a cheap EU enlargement," some of them added cynically.

[21] This initiative was actively supported by George Soros. See e.g., *Soros on Soros: Staying Ahead of the Curve*, Wiley and Sons, 1995.

[22] According to the *bon mot* by Bronislaw Geremek, the Accession lies always five years ahead of us.

[23] For ironic and angry responses from Eastern Europe to the paper by Jürgen Habermas and Jacques Derrida in *FAZ* on May 31, 2003, see Peter Esterhazy, "Wie groß ist der europäische Zwerg?," *Süddeutsche Zeitung* 2003/6/11, and Ivan Krastev, "Nicht ohne mein Amerika," *Die Zeit*, 2003/8/14.

[24] See József Böröcz, "Empire and Coloniality in the 'Eastern Enlargement' of the European Union," in: *Empire's New Clothes. Unveiling EU Enlargement, Central Europe Review,* e-book, 2001. See also Krzysztof Pomian, "Vor der Osterweiterung: Westliche Vorurteile, polnische Ängste," *Transit* 2003/25.

[25] See my "Westerweiterung ..." In one of the interviews the Polish team conducted in the framework of IWM's project "After the Accession ..." I read the following lines: "I remember that once I picked up tomatoes and I did not feel like working, I was very fucked up, too and made a kind of historical analysis, whether he, my employer, does not have some obligations toward me as a Pole because they in 1945 had left us... I was getting more and more

angry with this man ... OK, if I were a student and worked there, it would be OK but I work there because I cannot earn money in my own country, I am a poor man here in this Holland, of course, because they abandoned us, they had sold us to the Russians ..." (I am grateful to Jacek Kochanowicz for calling my attention to this text.)

[26] The populists are mistaken. True, Article 42, the so-called solidarity clause, in the EU draft constitution is rather empty (by and large, it refers to mutual assistance in times of terrorist attacks and natural disaster) but at least it does not hide ulterior motives.

[27] See my comments in *Transit* 2002/25 on Alfred Gusenbauer's programmatic paper on populism.

[28] "Can one create social cohesion within the nation states, without creating cohesion between them?", they wondered.

[29] Andrei Plesu addresses the West with melancholy: "Look ... we got out of historical mess ... We turned ugly, tired and became sour. We bare all the sins of the prodigal son, we return to you, full of wounds but of hopes, too. Where is the golden calf? ... Maybe you would say you are not obliged to nourish us in expensive sanatoriums, to heal us." ("Die verlorenen Söhne und ihre Sünden. Welchen Patriotismus braucht Europa? Warum die Länder Osteuropas fürchten, ihre Originalität zu verlieren," in: *Süddeutsche Zeitung* June 5, 1997).

[30] Cf. the recent initiative by Brussels called "Wider Europe."

[31] According to Heather Grabbe, "the nightmare scenario is ten new member states which behave like Spain on the budget, but like Britain and Denmark in their Euroscepticism." (*CER Bulletin,* Issue 5, August/September 2002).

[32] The entrants had to accept that they would get much less than the beneficiaries of the "Southern Enlargement". To compare, in 2000, for example, Portugal, Ireland and Greece received 200 to 400 euros per capita from Brussels, while for the newcomers the EU will offer no more than 30 to 70 euros per year and per capita in the period between 2004 and 2006. In the period between 2000 and 2006, 67 billion euros will be spent by Brussels for the Enlargement: this amounts to one thousandth of the GDP of the EU and one tenth of what the former GDR received during 1990–1999 (see Heather Grabbe, *Profiting from EU Enlargement,* CER, London 2001).

[33] The reaction by Jacques Chirac to the "letter of eight" demonstrates how fast indifference can turn into an angry talking-to if the entrants replace resentment by rational coalition-building.

[34] "Today we have 2 apples for 15 persons, unfortunately, tomorrow we will have only 1 for 25 but no one asked you to eat apples," said an Austrian politician to me in a private conversation.

[35] Interestingly enough, when it comes to a comparison with the US, the EU prefers to distinguish itself by pointing to its own greater sensitivity in social matters.

[36] Today, the old slogan of the dissidents "return to Europe" appears in the declarations of leading politicians in Western Europe with a twisted meaning. Accordingly, the entrants are strongly requested to return to Europe (not from the Soviet empire but) from America. The "New Europe" is hesitating...

JACQUES RUPNIK

The European Union's Enlargement to the East and Solidarity

The word "solidarity" has been severely battered about by recent European history. It is part of both the Christian and Socialist traditions. The Communists' use, and abuse, of the term has largely contributed to its discrediting, with officially proclaimed solidarity becoming identified with the privileges of the ruling caste, while the term "brotherly help" was used to describe the occupation of a country with a different understanding of socialism. The first historical irony was when a Polish workers' movement in 1980 again gave "solidarity" a good name and rescued it from the so-called United Polish Workers Party (every word in the title being seen by *Solidarnosc* members as a lie). That rehabilitation of the word by Walesa's followers and Tischner's writings was of significance for the whole of Europe. And if the European Union is seeking inspiration, this remains as good a source as any.

The second great historical irony was that, after the collapse of communism, Chicago school free market economic liberalism was introduced in Poland under the banner of a trade union called Solidarity! The third irony, again with a Polish twist, came with the European Union's enlargement to the East and its "historic" summit in Copenhagen on 13 December 2002. The date coincided with the anniversary of General Jaruzelski's coup against Solidarity in December 1981. It was therefore tempting for the Polish prime minister, Leszek Miller, to point to the long road "from Polish Solidarity to European solidarity." Yet the slogan had a somewhat hollow ring to it. First, because Miller himself was no freedom fighter, but belonged to the Communist apparatus that brought down the Solidarity movement. And second because "European solidarity" was nowhere to be seen at the Copenhagen Summit, which displayed the triumph of the accountant's approach to enlargement to public opinion throughout Europe for the first time.

Indeed, the issue of the cost and the terms of including new members confronts the EU with a question about the future: can it do for Eastern Europe what it has done with such impressive success for Southern Europe? The second, no less important, question concerns the future of a distinct European social and economic model in an enlarged EU. The first issue raises criticisms and fears among the new members from the East. The second raises concerns particularly among the Union's "old" founding members.

European solidarity, the costs of enlargement and asymmetrical integration

In the process of reconnecting with Western Europe, along with the prospect of belonging to the community of democratic nations, there were two other expectations in Central and Eastern Europe: modernization and solidarity. The Spanish model was present in the minds of Polish (and other) political elites not just for its negotiated transition to democracy, but because Europe had contributed so much to the transformation of a backward rural country emerging from four decades of dictatorship into a prosperous, modern nation, fully integrated into the mainstream of the European Union. Hence the question in Central European minds: Could the EU do for them what it had done so successfully for Southern Europe? The answer is probably not, or certainly not on a comparable scale.

One need only compare the modest resources made available. The 10 new countries have 75 million inhabitants, making up nearly one third of the EU's territory, but account for less than 5% of the EU's combined GDP. If the Copenhagen terms of enlargement are anything to go by, the prospects of correcting this imbalance are rather limited. The total planned expenditure for the period 2004–2006 is 40 billion euros, from which more than one third should be deducted to account for the newcomers' contributions to the EU budget and their difficulties in qualifying for EU regional funds. This leads the author of a recent study commissioned by Jacques Delors' think tank

"*Notre Europe*" to conclude that "the amounts allocated to the 10 candidate countries are in no way comparable to the much more generous terms granted to Spain and Portugal" in the mid-1980's.

This state of affairs prompts three related observations. First, it challenges the prevailing concept of a "light" enlargement, i.e. the idea that you can expand to include a dozen poor countries while upholding the sacrosanct "doctrine" of an EU budgetary limit set at 1.27% of the EU's GDP (which is currently no more than 1%). The question of solidarity and the EU budget thus inevitably raises the issue of Europe's fiscal capacity to create transfers of wealth. This in turn would involve the European Parliament having a say on the level of budgetary resources, and not just as to how they are used.

The second issue is that solidarity is closely related to policy reform. This applies to both agricultural policy (CAP) and the so-called Structural Funds. The agricultural policy makes up about 45% of the EU budget for 4% of the population, and a mere 2% of the EU's GDP. If the policy is not reformed for the sake of solidarity in the context of enlargement to the East, then it should be reformed for the sake of solidarity with the Third World countries seeking access to EU markets.

The third point concerns the strengthening and redefinition of the cohesion policies. A report for the President of the EU Commission, presented by André Sapir on behalf of a group of policy advisers in July 2003, clearly argues for an eastward reorientation of those policies to benefit those most needing them. This directly challenges the present beneficiaries, principally Spain, which now gets over one third of the funds, and Greece which gets about one fifth, but also Portugal and Ireland. But it is precisely those who have benefited most from European solidarity over the past 20 years who are least eager to share with their "poor relations" on the Danube.

The enlargement to the East is a case of asymmetrical integration. The asymmetry has facilitated the transfer of norms and institutional convergence, but not a commensurate transfer of resources. In this the EU's *function of regulation* takes precedence over the *function of redistribution*. Yet the regulatory function is likely to be accepted as legitimate by the newcomers from Central and Eastern Europe if it remains to some extent related to redistribution. Otherwise, cynics may be tempted to conclude that this is a case of "the less there is to distribute, the more there is to regulate."

The viability of a European social and economic model post-enlargement

It has often been argued that a European social and economic model combining competitiveness and solidarity has become an important part of the identity and cohesion of the EU, distinguishing it from the American (or Anglo-Saxon) free market model.[1] A specifically European response to the challenges of globalization is founded on the idea that there are certain spheres of social life—such as healthcare, education, the environment or culture—which should not simply be left to market forces. And it can indeed be argued that post-war European integration has developed in parallel with the welfare state in its Member States.[2] In fact, the European social model is part and parcel of the identity of the EU Member States more than of the EU per se.

Some scholars, like Claus Offe, have even argued that the EU has eroded the welfare state. That fear is clearly present in a number of EU Member States, particularly in the Nordic countries, as witnessed by recent referenda in Denmark or Sweden. Hence the question: what is the future of that social model in the face of the combined challenges of globalization and EU enlargement?

There is a fairly widespread assumption or apprehension that the newcomers from Central and Eastern Europe are mostly liberal free-marketers, who have spent the last decade dismantling the remnants of state socialism, making them unlikely to identify with the so-called "European social and economic model" inherited from Western European Social and Christian Democrats. To be sure, it was Milton Friedman and Margaret Thatcher, rather than Jacques Delors or the SPD manifesto, who provided the inspiration for Leszek Balcerowicz and Václav Klaus in shaping the transition to capitalism. And it is also true that most of the new members tend to oppose any EU regulation on taxation and social norms in order, quite understandably, to retain their comparative advantage for Western investors.

The short answer to those who voice such concerns is that the "Rhineland model" is no longer a model (with zero growth and 10% unemployment). The only way to preserve a "European social model" is to enlarge it eastwards. And the only way to do that is to reform it in the West.

There are, however, two factors that could help the EU move in that direction. Most of the reasons—such as demographic decline and the implosion of health care and pension systems—why the post-war European social system is bursting at the seams are now common to both the old and new EU members. The Czech or Hungarian populations are declining in the same way as those of Spain or Italy and the pressures for reform are very similar. No less importantly, whatever the differences of policies pursued by the so-called old and new Europeans, they are not confirmed by public opinion in their respective countries. According to the 2003 report of the Pew Global Attitudes Project,[3] there is in fact a fair amount of convergence between Central and Eastern Europe and Western Europe on the major issues concerning the relationship between the market and a social safety net guaranteed by the State. There remains an underlying commitment to a reformed version of a "social market economy."

The old European social model is in tatters. Its reform, or rather its re-invention, involves redefining what solidarity is supposed to mean at the beginning of the 21st century. Its only chance may be as a joint endeavor between the old and new Union members.

The erosion of solidarity and the political bond

The historical sequence of Western democracies outlined by Thomas H. Marshall—from civil rights and the rule of law in the 18th century to political rights and representative democracy in the 19th century to social rights based on solidarity in the 20th century—has some relevance for European integration as well: from the "*acquis communautaire*" and the rule of law to a quest for democratic legitimacy beyond that derived from the Member States, and for solidarity (reducing differences between Member States through re-distribution).

This pattern has been eroding since the end of the Cold War, primarily on the level of *internal solidarity* within states (between rich and poor regions). This was a contributing factor (though not necessarily a decisive one) in the break-up of Yugoslavia and of Czechoslovakia. One of the features of Alpine populism, including Bossi's Northern League in Italy, Blocher's movement in Switzerland and Haider's in Austria is the rejection of redistribution to poorer neighbors/foreigners. But this trend also applies to *external solidarity*. The growing disinclination to help developing countries is a clear illustration.

It is in that context that one can also analyze the erosion of solidarity in the enlarged European Union. There are a variety of reasons for this in Western Europe, ranging from lack of vision and leadership by European leaders unable to formulate a long-term European project in which the new "other European" members would be seen as a positive contribution to the narrow corporatist interests of this or that section of society. The latter defend the status quo, playing on their constituencies' egoism and fears. But there are also some specific Central and Eastern European contributions to that process:

1. To be a committed advocate of the free market does not necessarily help you to argue the case for re-distribution on a European level with Western European interlocutors (let alone public opinion).

2. The new members from Central and Eastern Europe tend to see and present the EU as primarily an economic institution, as opposed to NATO, which is primarily political and based on common values. If that is the case, then there is little point or credibility in invoking EU solidarity.

3. It is difficult to advocate "solidarity" in the EU when so little of it has been evident among Central Europeans in the past decade. Once they are in the EU, will they advocate greater solidarity with the poor and downtrodden future candidates from the Balkans? And yet this is perhaps where EU solidarity is most needed, not just as a moral obligation, but also out of obvious self-interest.

4. At the end of the day, solidarity can only be based on a political bond. In siding so resolutely with the US against "old Europe" in the transatlantic crisis (regardless of the intrinsic merits or otherwise of the Iraq war), the Central and Eastern European EU members have, along with others, contributed to undermining the political bonds within the enlarged EU. The moment of Europe's unification was obviously that of its division. Among the first casualties are public support for EU enlargement and the will to demonstrate (in concrete terms) solidarity with new members. Their security interests might well lie with the US, but their long-term economic interests are clearly with the EU. The political elites of these countries have failed to fully appreciate the implications of their stance.

The pattern of redistribution after enlargement observed in the case of Southern Europe (around 5% of GDP) is unlikely to be repeated in the case of Central and Eastern Europe. In the former case, redistribution was related not just to lofty ideas of solidarity after emerging from dictatorship, but also to the ability of small newcomers to block big projects. With the enlargement and a new Constitution, the EU is completing its last major project. The absence of "major projects," combined with the end of unanimity (and along with it, the end of blackmail), is also likely to herald the end of major redistribution.

Differences on foreign policy issues, on the extent of redistribution, or on the design of institutions are a normal part of the political debate in the European Union. What could be worrying for the future of the EU is an overlap between the divisions at work in the transatlantic relations, the Constitution elaborated by the European Convention, and the European social and economic model. It is very important to avoid such an overlap in the perceptions of elites and of public opinion if we want to avoid the hardening of a European divide and wish instead to see the word "solidarity" retain its meaning at the heart of the European project.

Notes

[1] Cf. Michel Albert, *Capitalisme contre capitalisme*, Paris, 1992.

[2] Cf. Dominique Schnapper, *La democratie providentielle,* Paris, 2002.

[3] "Views of a Changing World, June 2003", Washington (www.people-press.org).

KURT BIEDENKOPF, BRONISLAW GEREMEK,
KRZYSZTOF MICHALSKI and MICHEL ROCARD

What Holds Europe Together?

Concluding Remarks*

1. The European Union now faces perhaps the greatest challenge in
its history. It is expanding—dramatically so—with more than 70 million people becoming eligible for new European passports this year.
Simultaneously with this expansion, the Union is attempting to transform itself into a new type of political entity, as it radically redefines
itself through the process of drafting and ratifying a constitution.

The Union's expansion, bringing in ten new member countries,
also brings into the Union people who are often much poorer and culturally vastly different from the majority of the citizens in the older
Member States. The vast majority of these new EU citizens, many of
whom endured decades of subjugation to Communist regimes, hold
thoughts and values indelibly marked by experiences unfamiliar to
long-time EU citizens. As a result, economic and cultural differences
within the Union have, at a stroke, become much greater and more
intense. The constitutional process to define the Union in a more
ambitious way fuels this intensity to an even greater degree.

Faced with *growing diversity* and the rigors of establishing a
more demanding kind of unity, what forces can hold the expanded,
redefined European Union together? What moral concepts, what
traditions, what goals are capable of bringing together the Union's
diverse inhabitants in a democratic polity, and thereby underpinning
and anchoring the European constitution?

To examine these questions Romano Prodi, the President of the
European Commission, appointed academics and politicians from a
number of Union member countries to reflect on the intellectual and
cultural dimension of an EU in the process of enlargement—in par-

ticular to consider the relevance of this dimension to the cohesion of the expanded and redefined Union.

2. *Hitherto* the Union has been enormously successful. It established durable bonds, which made a European civil war virtually impossible. The Union established a zone of peace founded on *freedom, the rule of law,* and *social justice.* Within its Member States the Union speeded the task of overcoming the economic consequences of the Second World War, promoting reconstruction and, later, unprecedented affluence across Europe.

Economic integration and the gradual abolition of national economies led the way to this peaceful order. After the First World War, the French army occupied the Ruhr in order to prevent a revival of German heavy industry. After the Second World War, the French and the Germans decided to integrate their coal and steel industries. In doing so they laid the foundation for a lasting European peace.

3. A strong political will in the six founding states was needed both to make this development possible and to sustain it. Such a will was possible because of several factors that encouraged integration: the profound and widespread *shock of the Second World War;* the mounting *threat posed by the Soviet Union,* and the *economic dynamism* released by the founding of the Union's precursor, the European Economic Community (EEC), and further enhanced by the integration of national economies.

4. As memories of the Second World War faded and the risk of conflict between the Atlantic Alliance and the Soviet Union receded, the transformation of the EEC into the European Community, and finally into the European Union, pushed the Union's economic goals ever more to the fore. Economic growth, improvement in living standards, extending and enhancing systems of social protection, and rounding off the common market assumed priority.

But given the growing number of Member States, economic and social differences expanded—as did the expectations of EU citizens. Over time, it became increasingly evident that economic integration—no matter how important it and its political consequences may be—is incapable of substituting for the political forces that originally propelled European integration and cohesion.

This is why the aims formulated a few years ago by the Lisbon Council—to make Europe the most competitive economic region in the world by 2010, to establish a labor participation rate of 70%, and to bring about lasting growth, affluence, and social justice—have effectively disappeared from public consciousness. Not only have these goals been overtaken by events; they also have done nothing to bring Europeans closer together. They do not and cannot establish the internal cohesion that is necessary for the European Union; nor, indeed, can economic forces alone provide cohesion for any political identity. To function as a viable and vital polity, the European Union needs a firmer foundation.

It is no coincidence that economic integration is not enough to drive European political reform. Economic integration simply does not, of itself, lead to political integration because *markets cannot produce a politically resilient solidarity*. Solidarity—a genuine sense of civic community—is vital because the competition that dominates the marketplace gives rise to powerful centrifugal forces. Markets may create the economic basis of a polity, and are therefore an indispensable condition of its political constitution. But they cannot on their own produce the Union's political integration. The original expectation that the EU's political unity would be a consequence of the European common market has proven illusory.

Indeed, the current debate over the reform of the Union's Growth and Stability Pact shows once again that economic integration, symbolized by the launching of the Euro, can only continue as a basis of Europe's peaceful order if it is followed by deeper political integration within the Union. A currency union means a common economic policy. But when the forces of cohesion based on shared economic successes wane or are overshadowed by internal competition, a common economic policy requires political integration, i.e. a level of internal cohesion that remains effective even when economic interests diverge.

So Europe's political union demands *political cohesion*, a politically grounded community bound by ties of solidarity. Both the future of the Union and the dimensions of its political integration will be decided by whether these political forces of cohesion exist, and whether they prove to be adequate to times of crisis.

5. Recognizing this, the countries of the European Union deliberately set out on the path of political integration. The Union's constitutional process expresses this decision. But how much political integration is necessary and how politically potent should the Union become? *To what end* does the Union need the *political ability to act?*

First, because an economic order never evolves in a value-free environment. It requires a legal framework and protection, the development of necessary institutions, and the state's enforcement of standards and duties forged and agreed among by the people. An effective and just economic order must also be embedded in the morals, customs, and expectations of human beings, as well as in their social institutions. So, the manner in which the larger European economic area—the common market—is in harmony with the values of European citizens, as varied as these may be, is no mere academic problem; it is a fundamental and political one. The constant need to make Europe's political expression reflect the values of Europe's citizens is as significant as the functioning of that common market itself.

Second, this task, the full extent of which became evident with the completion of the common market, requires political institutions with legislative, administrative, and judicial functions. Only by developing such institutions (for example, a structure of economic governance that can manage the currency union) and assuring their political legitimacy, can a viable and vital political entity be created. The Union's constitutional process and the subsequent adoption of the European constitutional treaty will, it is expected, provide lasting legitimacy for the institutional framework of a politically constituted Europe. The constitutional treaty is intended to define the Union's political unity.

Third, the Union also needs the political ability to act because it confronts a myriad of new tasks:

- overcoming the consequences of Europe's aging population;
- managing, both politically and legally, the desire of people from around the globe to immigrate into the Union;
- dealing with the increasing inequality that is the direct result of increased immigration, as well as of the Union's expansion;
- preserving peace in a globalized world.

6. So where are the forces of cohesion for the new political Union to be found if the common interests produced by economic integration are no longer sufficient? We believe that the older forces that animated European unification are no longer sufficiently powerful to provide genuine political cohesion, and that, therefore, *new sources of energy must be looked for and found in Europe's common culture.*

This does not, of course, mean that the powers that have served until now will play no role in the future. But what *has* changed today is the *relative significance* of the existing forces of cohesion, and their relative contribution to the future unity of Europe. As the old forces of integration—the desire for peace, the existence of external threats, and the potential for economic growth—lose their effectiveness, the role of Europe's common culture—the spiritual factor of European integration—will inevitably grow in importance as a source of unity and cohesion.

At the same time, the meaning of European culture needs to be better understood and made politically effective. A mere list of common European values is not enough to serve as the basis of European unity, even if the charter of basic rights included in the Union's constitutional treaty points in this direction. This is so because every attempt to codify "European values" is inevitably confronted with a variety of diverging national, regional, ethnic, sectarian, and social understandings. A constitutional treaty cannot eliminate this diversity of interpretation, even if backed up by legislation and judicial interpretation.

Still, despite such difficulties of definition, there can be no doubt that there exists a common European cultural space: a variety of traditions, ideals, and aspirations, often intertwined and at the same time in tension with one another. These traditions, ideals, and aspirations bring us together in a shared context and make us "Europeans": citizens and peoples capable of a political unity and a constitution that we all recognize and experience as "European."

This common European cultural space cannot be firmly defined and delimited; its borders are necessarily open, not because of our ignorance, but in principle—because European culture, indeed Europe itself, is not a "fact": *it is a task and a process.*

What is European culture? What is Europe? These are questions that must be constantly posed anew. So long as Europe is of the present, and not simply the past, they can never be conclusively answered.

Europe's identity is something that must be negotiated by its peoples and institutions. Europeans can, and must, adapt themselves and their institutions, so that European values, traditions, and conceptions of life can live on and be effective. At the same time, the Union and its citizens must make their values endure as a basis of common identity through ever-changing conditions.

Europe and its cultural identity thus depend on a constant confrontation with the new, the other, the foreign. Hence the question of European identity will be answered in part by its immigration laws, and in part by the negotiated accession terms of new members. Neither of these—either the immigration laws or the terms of accession—can be determined *a priori* on the basis of fixed, static definitions, such as a catalogue of "European values."

7. If Europe is not a fact, but a task, neither can there be any fixed, eternally defined, European boundaries, be they internal or external. Europe's boundaries, too, must always be renegotiated. It is not geographical or national borders, then, that define the European cultural space—it is rather the latter which defines the European geographical space, a space that is in principle open.

This also means that the common *European cultural space cannot* be defined *in opposition to national cultures*. Polish farmers and British workers should not see "European culture" as something foreign or even threatening. For the same reason, European culture *cannot* be defined *in opposition to a particular religion* (such as Islam). What constitutes the content of "European culture" is not a philosophical question that can be answered *a priori*; nor is it a merely historical question. It is a question that calls for political decisions that attempt to demonstrate the significance of tradition in the face of future tasks that Europe's Union must address.

8. European culture, that open space that must be forever redefined, does not, in and of itself, establish European unity. That unity also requires a political dimension and the decisions that it engenders. But the common European culture is what gives politics the opportunity to make Europe into a unified political entity.

The unity of Europe is *not*, however, *only a political task*. Politics can create only the basic conditions for European unification. Europe itself is far more than a political construct. It is a complex—a "culture"—of institutions, ideas and expectations, habits and feelings, moods, memories and prospects that form a "glue" binding Europeans together. And all these are a foundation on which a political construction must rest. This complex—we can speak of it as *European civil society*—is at the heart of political identity. It defines the conditions of successful European politics, and also the limits of state and political intervention.

In order to foster the cohesion necessary for political unity, European politics must support the emergence and development of a civil society in Europe. It is through these institutions of civil society that our common European culture can become a reality. But this also means that politics and state institutions must be ready to recognize their limits.

This self-limitation implies that the political culture of Europe must be compatible with the sense of community rooted in a common European culture. To lay claim to a common European culture and history as the basis of political identity, European political institutions must live up to the expectations engendered by the European cultural tradition. In particular, the exercise of political power must be based on persuasive and transparent political leadership, rather than express itself as bureaucratic action of questionable legitimacy. Decentralization of public discussion and the processes of decision-making are especially important. Indeed, only decentralization can do justice to the cultural variety and the wealth of forms of social organization that make up European civil society.

9. If the countries of Europe are to grow together into a viable political union, the people of Europe must be prepared for *European solidarity*. This solidarity must be stronger than the universal solidarity that binds (or should bind) all human beings together, and that underlies the idea of humanitarian aid.

European solidarity—the readiness to open one's wallet and to commit one's life to others because they, too, are Europeans—is not something that can be imposed from above. It must be more than *institutional solidarity*. Europeans as individuals must feel it. When *individual solidarity* is not there, institutionally based solidarity is not enough to bring a polity into being.

The cultural, intellectual, economic, and political tendencies of recent decades—not least of all the advance of individualism—have led to an erosion of many forms of social solidarity. The crisis of the welfare state may be understood as a consequence of this development. This erosion may also be felt in the context of the recent European enlargement: it is reflected in the diminished willingness among the citizens of older member countries—in comparison with earlier expansions—to lend a hand, economically and politically, to the newcomers.

Strengthening of pan-European solidarity is one of the most important long-term tasks of European politics. In trying to accomplish this task, we should not labor under the illusion that the need for solidarity can be satisfied by institutional measures alone. Rather, all institutional measures must be sustained by the readiness of the population to manifest their own spirit of solidarity. It is thus important to give solidarity an active and prospective, rather than passive and retrospective, dimension: we must define it in terms of the new common tasks that Europe must address—rather than with respect to past achievements in sharing our wealth with the existing members of the Union.

10. A particular challenge for European solidarity arises from the expansion of the Union to countries previously forming part of the Soviet empire. How we deal with this challenge will be decisive for the future of Europe.

How will this expansion alter the conditions of European solidarity? What do the new members bring to the common table? Will they, as many fear, be mainly spoilers, and will they—traumatized by totalitarianism and lacking a strong Enlightenment tradition—slow down, or even bring to a halt, the process of the Union's democratization? Will they, because of their historically and strategically determined closeness to the United States, frustrate Europe's aspirations to a common foreign policy? Or will the new members not only expose the Union to new dangers, but also open it up to new opportunities?

The year 1989 ushered Europe into a new age. It did not merely make possible the enlargement of Europe to the former Communist East. It also enriched Europe. That is why the new members, despite their economic weakness, should be taken into the Union as equal partners. They should be able to shape the new Union along with the old members. And we must also look for the European element in their traditions and experiences.

That the European Union was given, in 1989, a historic opportunity of rebirth was in large part due to the revolutionary uprisings of people in Communist-ruled Eastern Europe. The East European rev-

olutions were proof of the strength of the *solidarity of a civil society.*
They are the best evidence that true political realism must take the
existence of these bonds into account—and not merely those interests writ in the stone and mortar of political institutions.

11. In the search for forces capable of establishing cohesion and
identity in the European Union, the question of the *public role of
European religions* is particularly important.

Over the last few centuries, European democratic societies, learning from tragic experience, have attempted to remove religion from
the political sphere. Religion was considered, with good reason, as
divisive, rather than conciliatory. That may still be the case today. But
Europe's religions also have the potential to bring people in Europe
together, instead of separating them.

We believe that the presence of religion in the public sphere cannot be reduced to the public role of the churches, or to the societal
relevance of explicitly religious views. Religions have long been an
inseparable component of the various cultures of Europe. They are
active "beneath the surface" of political and state institutions; they
also have an effect on society and individuals. The result is a new
wealth of religious forms entwined with cultural meanings.

Even in Europe, where modernization and secularization appear
to go hand in hand, public life without religion is inconceivable. The
community-fostering power of Europe's religious faiths should be
supported and deployed on behalf of the cohesion of the new Europe.
The risks involved, however, should not be overlooked. These include a
possible invasion of the public sphere by religious institutions, as well
as the threat that religion may be used to justify ethnic conflicts. It
must be remembered that many apparent religious conflicts have political or social causes, and that they may be solved by social measures
before they become religiously charged.

The questions concerning the public role of religion in Europe
resurfaced recently because of the Balkan wars, the Muslim immigration into Europe, and (thus far less dramatically) the prospect of
Turkey's becoming an EU member. The question of the *political relevance of Islam* comes to the forefront in this connection.

To be sure, it is hard to deny that the increasing presence of the
various forms of Islam in Europe's public space poses both new
opportunities and new dangers for European integration. It potential-

ly calls into question the prevailing ideas about public space. Among European Moslems, there is a tendency to detach religion from the specific cultural and social context of their homelands, and this may have potentially dangerous consequences. But the only feasible path toward a solution of the problems posed by Islam in Europe consists in understanding the consequences of transplanting Islam into a European context, rather than in a frontal confrontation between the abstractions of "Christian Europe" and "Islam."

12. What is the impact of the intellectual and cultural meaning of Europe on *Europe's role in the world*? To the extent that Europe acknowledges the values inherent in the rules that constitute European identity, those very same values will make it impossible for Europeans not to acknowledge their duty of solidarity toward non-Europeans. This globally defined solidarity imposes on Europe an obligation to contribute, in accordance with its ability, to the securing of world peace and the fight against poverty. But despite this global calling, there can be no justification for attempting to impose, perhaps with the help of the institutions of a common European foreign and defense policy, any specific catalogue of values on other peoples.

The fundamental dilemma of European foreign policy is the tension between the logic of peace and the logic of cohesion. Europe sees itself as both a *zone of peace* and *a community of values*. This dilemma cannot be solved *a priori*. There is no essence of Europe, no fixed list of European values. There is no "finality" to the process of European integration.

Europe is a project of the future. With every decision, not only its zone of peace, its institutions, its political, economic and social order, but also its very identity and self-determination are opened to questioning and debate. In principle this has been the case throughout Europe's history. Europe's capacity for constant change and renewal was, and remains, the most important source of its success and its unique character. This source must always be recognized anew and given institutional form: through European politics, through civil society, and through the force of European culture. In the end, it all comes to this: we must sustain and use our European heritage, and not allow it to perish.

October 2004

* Further referred to as "Europe Paper."

Comments

SAMUEL ABRAHÁM

Needed but Uncertain Cohesion

It was a pleasure to read a sober yet hopeful assessment of the condition Europe finds itself at the present. It is both a relevant analysis for European politicians as well as an intellectual challenge so needed in the contemporary, often cynical, often superficial discourse about all things European. A remark from the text could become a motto for the EU in the best of our enlightenment and liberal traditions: "There is no essence of Europe, no fixed list of European values. There is no 'finality' to the process of European integration." (A cheer for the triple negative—a perfect pendant to the American "In God We Trust.")

I perceive the future of the EU as primarily a political enterprise, and for me the key questions in the paper are to what extent "political integration is necessary and how politically potent should the Union become? To what end does the Union need the political ability to act?" We do not know, and in fact it is impossible to say at this moment, yet these are crucial questions. Certainly, spiritual and cultural cohesion is necessary but they certainly do not provide an answer regarding the degree of 'freedom of political action' needed for EU executive and legislative powers.

The authors stress that economics is no longer the source of unity. It neither delivers prosperity as it did before—certainly not uniformly—nor can it become a cohesive force in a highly diverse and evolving Europe. Europe needs political cohesion based not on a common market, they argue, but one fortified by other attributes such as shared culture, solidarity, and institutions of civil society, as well as by an enhanced role for European religions. They are sober in their assessment when they stress that "both the future of the Union and the dimensions of its political integration will be decided by whether these political forces of cohesion exist and whether they prove to be adequate in times of crisis." Hence they are aware that there is no direct or inevitable transition to replace economics with other forces that bolster political cohesion. Yet elsewhere they state that Europe's common culture "will inevitably grow in importance as a source of unity and cohesion." This, however, is not *inevitable*, only desirable.

The point is that if, in the past, political integration was fortified by economics, it is not clear whether stressing the centrality of solidarity, along with spiritual and cultural dimensions, will provide political cohesion to a future Europe. I want to highlight this inconsequential relation by focusing on certain paradoxes that have shaped the development of the EU and are relevant to the current debate.

Just for the sake of argument, let's simplify and say that the pinnacle of the pre-expansion period was the establishment of the common currency—an expression of the confidence and trust in the EU as a viable economic unit. The EU members were ready to risk giving up their national currencies—their ultimate economic protector and symbol. There was no intellectual, spiritual or cultural component involved in introducing the Euro. Nor was there that much need for solidarity in a confident and prosperous European Union.

However, Europe's economy has been under increasing strain and it is a part of the EU's several predicaments (others are the preservation of welfare state, setting immigration policies and the admission of Turkey). Economic prosperity can thus no longer 'integrate' Europe. The wide economic disparity among various member states, as well as competition for limited resources and investments, can bring about strain that could threaten the EU's stability. Hence, another type of cohesion is necessary. From this point of view, it is paradoxical that while the EU is expanding and the former cohesion is under a threat, the focus is no longer on economics, but on cultural and spiritual dimensions that cannot provide the tangible protection and comfort a prosperous economy did before the expansion.

Another paradox, one might argue, is that intellectual, spiritual and cultural integration would have been more easily achievable in the past, yet were not attempted. In fact, the cultural and spiritual diversity of Europe was considered as an asset. Now that the diversity of the EU is broadening beyond the point of perceiving the EU as a natural unit—and would further do so if there were another round of expansion—there is both a moral and ethical appeal to Europeans to search for a new and common identity that had been assumed, but never explicitly cultivated. The risk is that, however positive in principle, relying on the cultural and spiritual dimension makes the whole enterprise vulnerable. It is not clear whether 1) it is useful, 2) whether it is attainable and 3) if it is attained, to what extent it would deliver actual political cohesion.

Finally, expansion of the EU and the entrance of the 11 new member states take place within a highly integrated yet fragile economic and political compact. Had these 11 new members entered during the southern expansion two decades ago, most likely there would be no need to stress cultural and spiritual cohesion now. What would have had mattered then would have been economic discipline and the schedule of transferring structural funds in order to share and spread prosperity—institutional solidarity would have been sufficient. There would have been gradual legal and political harmonization, yet these would have been less dramatic than what we witnessed in the past several years. The final paradox is, then, that, as the EU diversifies and the expansion undermines and weakens its economic homogeneity, there is a call for something that is necessary, but more difficult to achieve than if it had been attempted in the past.

One realizes that bureaucrats are important because Europe is, among other things, a huge bureaucratic enterprise (to assure "political institutions with legislative, administrative, and judicial functions"). Yet bureaucrats cannot mold Europe into an organic unit. Similarly, politicians are important; in the end it is they who decide. Europe, however, should not become a playground where they play out their political ambitions. They should recognize, as the authors point out, that Europe is not a 'fact' but above all 'a task and a process.'

European bureaucrats and politicians would have to incorporate into their mindset the idea that political integration and the degree of its legitimacy depend on the depth of cultural and spiritual cohesion, and on solidarity among Europeans. And this is an intellectual challenge and goal that is neither inevitable, nor one that would result from routine political deliberation. One contribution towards this goal is the reflection summarized in the Europe Paper. In the end, the key question is whether the politicians will pay only lip service to the conclusions of the analysis, or whether the authors' worthy effort can become a strategy for a new Europe.

GIULIANO AMATO

Building Europe

The document written by Kurt Biedenkopf, Bronislaw Geremek, Krzysztof Michalski and Michel Rocard goes straight to the crucial dilemma that is confronting Europe. And the instruments that its authors suggest in order to face the dilemma (if not necessarily solve it) reveal an unusual and deep understanding of our "unity in diversity" and of the means by which to draw the best out of its potentialities.

The dilemma is not a new one, but it has a new dimension in the enlarged Europe: on one hand, the project of Europe as a new political entity based on common values, common goals and common rights enshrined in the Constitution; on the other, the increased diversity of our enlarged family, that might endanger the project. The project—it is argued—cannot rely on the common vision and the political will that supported the golden age of the initial integration of our market, for they seem to be exhausted. At the same time the Constitution, by redefining that vision for an enlarged Europe, envisages a sort of impossible mission, for it seems quite unlikely that the new and heterogeneous membership of Europe can express the new common vision that is needed.

Should this pessimistic view prevail, it could lead to consequences that are quite disturbing for our future: a lack of credibility for the Constitution, the return of old dreams—a *petite Europe* as the only political subject vs. the countries of enlargement as *espace economique* — and eventually the surrender to a view of our diversity as incompatible with any form of unity beyond economic matters. It is not an unlikely scenario; on the contrary, several signs tell us that it may come true. How to oppose it and where to find the resources and energies to preserve Europe (in its entirety) as a political project, albeit a renewed one?

The Europe Paper says, quite firmly, that the energies we need in support of cohesion must be looked for and found in our common European culture. Our European religions, which are inseparable components of our various cultures, can greatly contribute, not to divide people (as they did in the past), but to bring them together.

Is this a viable path to an ever-closer integration within our new context (and within an even broader one, that might include Turkey and the Balkans in a not distant future)? Culture is where we tend to differentiate from one another and it is a fact that Europe speaks more of "cultures" than of "culture." Precisely for this reason, a recent doctrine concerning the "constitutional patriotism" that might be common to an identifiable European people isolates such patriotism from our cultural, ethnic and national identities (I am referring here to Jürgen Habermas). If a political identity can unite us, this doctrine suggests, it has to be based on what we want to do together, not on the "pre-political" values that are typical of each of us. So, where is that "common European culture" and how can it provide the glue?

Here is where our document is really penetrating: in realizing that no list, nor codification, of European cultural values makes sense, and yet that a European culture does exist. It is a context with open borders, to which a constant confrontation with the new may provide, and actually does provide, verifiable contents, as long as a political leadership exists that is persuasive and convincing in exercising this task; for our common culture—the document says—is not a fact, but a task.

I personally agree with this analysis, which allows us, first of all, to become aware of the hidden but undeniable shortcomings of the doctrine on constitutional patriotism. The supposed underpinning of this kind of patriotism is purely political, Habermas argues, for culture would be divisive. But we cannot share the political will that is needed to support a European project on only the basis of common economic or political interests. If such a political will exists, it necessarily presupposes common cultural values, without which we can neither support nor accept the European architecture, the rule of law that is dominant within them.

This includes the definition, and protection, of all those individual rights that "our" rule of law has brought in its wake (the rule of law is not the same all over the world), and the common mission that Europe pursues. Similarly, the well-known doctrine by John Rawls as to the need for an exclusively "procedural" democracy whenever no agreement is feasible on a substantive notion of the common good actually implies some sort of substantive *entente*. Otherwise, not even an agreement on purely procedural rules would be feasible (and enforceable).

The challenging question is: what are the common cultural values that underpin our European political identity (and therefore the European construction) and how have they been acknowledged? It is here that the analysis of our document applies. The European construction has been, and will continue to be, a process during which it will continue to be the task of all European decision-makers to take further steps in expounding upon both their political and legal reasoning and the broader underpinnings of their philosophies.

Most of our common cultural values have been discovered and recognized throughout this process. No previous list of our rights existed when the European Court of Justice first decided in 1963 that we have rights against our own states. And since that first decision we have unanimously acknowledged the "constitutional traditions common to the Member States" as "general principles" of our common European law. How *not* to see here the distillation, out of different national cultures, of a common cultural denominator that is transformed into a set of common general principles?

Similarly, in 1993, we had no codification telling us that the protection of minority rights was an essential aspect of our common life. When the European Council, meeting in Copenhagen that year, approved the conditions for future accessions (the protection of minority rights among them), we discovered that it was. And so it has remained.

The examples can be multiplied (think of the death penalty, that our culture rejects, and which was written in the Charter of our Fundamental Rights), but the rule is already clear and confirms our starting point: *that our common culture is not a fact, but a task.* And, as long as that task is exercised, we discover and acknowledge something more to be added to what we have in common. Not even the

Charter of Fundamental Rights, to which legal force should shortly be given, will put an end to this crucial task. The Charter has been criticized as if it were a rigid and definite catalogue of values and rights, which would cause the process I have described to be paralyzed and frozen. It is not so. The process would only be paralyzed should Europe lose the unique character that has allowed it to flourish (when it has flourished), namely—as our document defines it—its capacity for constant development and renewal.

If this capacity remains, the Charter itself will be the source of future discoveries and acknowledgements. If it fades away, we will discover that our diversities are incompatible and that only "cultures" exist, with no common denominators among them. The delicate balance enshrined in our motto—"unity in diversity"—would go to pieces.

It is this delicate balance that preserves the European flavor of the continuously renewed blend of our common culture. And the process of enlargement, even in its future stages with Turkey and the Balkans, has no reason to be feared as a threat of dispossession, as long as its blend is enriched by the two-way input that safeguards the balance: on one hand, the diversities that comprise our family; on the other, the common values that affect the new members (who are simultaneously affected by their diversity) and hold all of us within the same flexible framework.

How can religions play a role in this complex process? Actually they *do* play a role, independently of any voluntary decision to do so, by their being inseparable components of our cultures (plural!), as has already been observed. The real question is whether they can combine to strengthen our magical balance, or to disrupt it by arming our diversities against one another. My point here is that they have extraordinary potential for strengthening the balance, and that it all depends on their leadership and on the men and women of good will who want that potential to be used positively.

The monotheistic religions of our region share one basic common principle: that all human beings are children of the same God. This one principle is (or, at least, should be) enough to oppose any use of religious differences as grounds for conflicting identities. Furthermore the ethical principles that are equally common to them—respect and even love for others, solidarity and a sense that our lives

cannot be narrowly restricted to the satisfaction of our selfish needs—
have a twofold and converging meaning.

Firstly, they are, by their very nature, not a divisive factor, but a
glue. Secondly, this specific glue is an essential antidote to the frag-
menting viruses that have been infecting our (Western) societies by
reducing the incentives for community life, enhancing the perceived
value of wealth and consumption, and separating our individual destinies from one another in the name of careers and prospects that
depend less and less on collective links and actions. From this viewpoint, I dare say that the support of religions is really indispensable
vis à vis the scarcity of other resources that we may use to neutralize
the same risks.

It is redundant to say that not even the expected benefits of religious beliefs and principles are facts; they too are the desirable fruits
of a task—a task that the repeated and structured dialogues among
religions have already undertaken, while the opposite is being done
by those political interests (sometimes disguised in religious gar-
ments) that use religion as a sword with which to stir ethnic conflict.
The future of a European common culture as a basic resource for the
cohesion of an enlarged and enlarging Europe depends very much on
the contest between these opposite roles of religion.

Should religion remain a domestic part of domestic cultures—
or, even worse, should it be instrumentally used to prove the incom-
patibility of compatible groups, countries or civilizations—the very
texture of Europe would be at risk. Should their principles and values be expounded according to their deepest and most truthful nature
(which includes their being intertwined with the prevailing cultures
of different countries), that texture would be enormously strengthened, and the sense of our magical balance between unity and diversity would also be enriched.

Europe is a wonderful construction, but it is also a never accom-
plished task, a challenge continuously confronting the generations
that follow each other throughout the years. The more Europe grows
and widens, the more its future cohesion depends on a wider arena,
not only of leaders, but of citizens, who have the attainment of that
cohesion in their hands. If we accept the conclusion that our common culture is the source from which the energy that keeps all of us
together has to be drawn, we must also accept the conclusion that we

ourselves are such a source, and that our leaders are responsible for the acknowledgement of the consequent implications. It is not an irrelevant conclusion in terms of an approach to Europe that might be expected from each and every one of us. To those who think that Europe is important to them, a once beloved American President would say: "Ask not what Europe can do for you, ask what you can do for Europe."

RAINER BAUBÖCK

Intersecting and Overlapping European Cultures

In 1882 the historian Ernest Renan gave a lecture at the Sorbonne on the topic 'What is a nation?' in which he stated laconically: "A customs union is not a fatherland." The European Union of today is more than a customs union, but certainly less than a fatherland. It also does not aspire to be, or to become, the latter. But it is assigning to itself ever more tasks whose completion had in the past required national solidarity. The basis of such solidarity has always been a sense of belonging to an imagined community of shared history and culture.

The Reflection Group on the spiritual and cultural dimension of Europe puts forward a diagnosis that resembles Renan's: "Markets cannot produce a politically resilient solidarity." And the group's reflections also start from the premise that "new sources of energy must be looked for and found in Europe's common culture." This raises several questions: What is the content of Europe's common culture? Where are its boundaries? How can it become a resource for political solidarity?

Many will have expected the Reflection Group to identify the roots of European culture or to proclaim a catalogue of essential European values. The group was wise enough to avoid this trap. On the one hand, any common list of historical roots (such as Greek democracy, Roman law, Christianity and the Enlightenment) is always meant to demarcate and exclude (e.g. Judaism and Islam). On the other hand, no catalogue of universal values (such as liberty, peace, the rule of law, democracy and solidarity) can claim to be European, not only in its origins, but also in grounding a specific European identity for the present and the future.

Instead of taking this much-traveled road, the concluding remarks published by the Reflection Group suggest that the questions "What is Europe?" and "What is European culture?" can never be conclusively answered. Europe's identity and borders are "something that must be negotiated by its peoples and institutions." European culture cannot be defined in contrast to either particular national cultures or religious beliefs. It is instead the culture of a civil society in which the public role of religion is also publicly recognized.

I agree with all of this. Yet there is something that is conspicuously absent. This is the theme of linguistic diversity. We should remember that, for modern nationalism since the French Revolution, the political community has been conceived primarily as a linguistic, not a religious, one. Europe, however, is multilingual to an extent that completely rules out any similar process of linguistic homogenization within the Union. In this respect it is different even from multilingual democracies, such as Canada, Belgium, Switzerland or India. India may have a greater number of languages than Europe, but in each of the countries mentioned there are no more than two or three official languages that are recognized within federal institutions.

The European Union today has already twenty such official languages. This language regime is costly—translation and interpreter services make up the largest part of the EU administrative budget—but it has so far not created a major obstacle for political integration. This is quite remarkable and illustrates the general insight that political unity in Europe—in stark contrast with national unity—does not require cultural unity with regard to either religion or language. The new Europe is instead a successful model for overcoming cultural conflict through recognizing diversity. And this is exactly the reason why any attempt to demarcate the cultural boundaries of Europe must ultimately endanger its unity.

Yet this seems to undercut the core thesis of the Reflection Group: that for the future tasks of the Union a shared culture will be the most important source of European solidarity. How is this common culture to be forged in the absence of state instruments for cultural homogenization that are unavailable at the European level? In the context of past nation-building, the perception that historically contingent borders of states coincide with stable cultural communities could only be made plausible through the coercive assimilation or ethnic cleansing of minorities, through establishing hegemonic national cultures in public education systems, and through geographic mobility in linguistically standardized labor markets.

The former two of these three means of nation-building are clearly excluded for the purposes of European integration. As far as the latter is concerned, there is some empirical evidence for the emergence of a new European elite that identifies with the integration project mainly because its members project their own career plans into this wider geographic space. For the great majority of Europeans, however, the continent with its multiple linguistic borders is a house in which each citizen feels at home in only one of its many rooms. Geographic mobility is a commodity that needs to be imported. While native middle classes remain largely immobile and distrustful of Europeanized elites, immigrants from third countries provide a mobile economic force whose job biographies and social networks create new transnational spaces. It is quite ironic that those who are still perceived as cultural aliens in Europe's nation-states could turn out to be the true Europeans of the future.

Since strong cultural unity in Europe can be brought about neither through state coercion nor through economic incentives, the only feasible and desirable goal is to strengthen the weak force of unity in diversity. If we drew a Venn diagram of European cultures, we could interpret the meaning of a shared culture in two different ways: either as an intersecting core shared by the various national, linguistic, secular and religious cultures, or as the "union set," i.e. the total ensemble formed by all these overlapping cultures.

For Eurosceptics, the intersecting set is too small in relation to the assigned task. I would, however, contend that the problem is just the opposite. In this core there are exactly those values listed above that may be European in their historical genesis, but that are universal in their content, and global in their contemporary reach. This core is quite strong and it is indeed of decisive importance for the political integration of Europe. It would be either naïve or disingenuous to claim that these values are actually shared by all European citizens, but they clearly manifest themselves in the political institutions and constitutions of both the Member States and the Union. The problem is that it is exactly the universalistic and institutional nature of such values that make them hardly suited as building blocks for a particular European identity that generates solidarity between its citizens.

As an alternative—or rather supplement—we must therefore consider the idea of an overlapping union in which the cultural diversity of Europe is understood as a connecting bond. When we take this second step, "colorless" European values will be tied together with a "colorful" identity. This identity will manifest the required traits of particularity, since it relates to the historically grown cultural differences within Europe. Such unity in diversity is not sufficiently expressed in the formula adopted by the 1997 Amsterdam Treaty: "The Union shall respect the national identities of its Member States." Cultural diversity could only become an anchor for European unity when it is no longer misinterpreted as a mosaic composed of monochrome nation-states.

Instead, Europe must learn to embrace the diversity within and across its internal political borders. One indicator of the distance that separates Europe from this goal is the fact that the Copenhagen criterion of respect for and protection of minorities has so far only been applied to accession candidates, but not to those who are already members of the club. Old Member States who regard this as their purely internal affair would block any move towards a pan-European regime of minority rights today. Developing minority rights standards has therefore been a task the Union has left to the Council of Europe, whose powers of enforcement are much more limited. This is another European cultural deficit that is, unfortunately, not considered by the Reflection Group.

Affirming universal values and diversity will not yet help to resolve the puzzle of Europe's borders. These can be fixed neither as natural nor as cultural ones. As the western peninsula of the Eurasian continent, Europe does not have any natural eastern borders. The Bosphorus is in this regard certainly no more natural as a divide than are the Ural Mountains. And any attempt to draw a boundary along linguistic or religious lines must conflict with the already existing diversity within present borders. Those who maintain that the strongly secularist Turkish state cannot belong to Europe because its societal culture has been shaped by Islam do not merely question shared European principles of religious freedom and the separation of church and state; they also deny the rights of approximately 15 million Muslims in the present Union to equal respect and access to full citizenship.

Yet every democratic polity needs borders, and so does Europe. If these are, as the Reflection Group suggests, a matter of negotiation, then the debate about their permeability for immigration and their openness to enlargement remains on the agenda. In deciding these questions, Europe will need to consider, on the one hand, consequences for European integration and, on the other, the legitimate expectations generated by past policies and promises towards particular groups of migrants and countries that want to join. As far as I can see, both considerations do not support policies of closing the doors either to Turkish accession or to future immigrants and refugees.

The bonding forces of European culture are in no way comparable with those unleashed by past and present projects of nation-building. But the supranational and multinational European project is also of an entirely different kind. It is still an open question whether the—admittedly weak—resources of universal values and openness to cultural diversity can mobilize sufficient solidarity for this project. But our experience over the past fifty years justifies at least the attempt to carry on.

JÁN ČARNOGURSKÝ

It is Necessary to Believe in Europe

The Europe Paper on the spiritual and cultural dimension of Europe correctly grasps the essential features of the phenomenon of Europe. Perhaps because it is a starting point for discussion, not its conclusion, it attempts to be neutral and restrained in its evaluation of individual aspects. When commenting on the report, it may be difficult to change the features of Europe it mentions, but the emphasis may be changed.

A change of emphasis enables us to mention the historic success of Europe, which brought it to the head of the other continents still at the beginning of their history. The source of European dynamism was internal tension, which continued throughout history, but changed its form. There was the tension between the Roman Empire and the barbarians, later between the Imperial power and the Church, then between the Catholic Church and Protestantism and, finally, between democracy and the totalitarian regimes. Further internal tensions in Europe could be named. They all produced the dynamism, which moved Europe forward.

The message of these chapters of European history teaches us that we should not fear internal tension in our continent, since we are probably permanently condemned to it. We do not have to fear it, because it can become a source of progress by creating space for free decisions. Internal tension also enables more rapid progress because it enables mutual destruction. The dividing line between more rapid progress and mutual destruction demarcates the ability to respect our opponent—not to attempt to destroy him, but to engage him in a chivalrous struggle. It should at least be chivalrous from our side, even if the opponent refuses to struggle in a chivalrous manner.

The challenge of an enlarged European Union lies in the fact that it joins into one unit, societies with different structures of internal relations. With some simplification, it is possible to say that in the west of our continent history formed societies that place greater emphasis on individualism, but that in the east greater emphasis is placed on collectivism. This difference will create obstacles to the acceptance of the decisions of the European Union. However, a source of optimism is that European nations or societies can agree with one another more easily than they could agree with non-European societies.

The family has an exceptional place in the structure of European societies, and within it the woman has a special position. The only thing that can be criticized in the report is that it is not concerned with the position of the family and women in European societies. The importance of the family in the societies of other continents can successfully compete with the importance of the family in Europe, but the exceptional character of the European family lies precisely in the position of the woman in the family. The woman holds the family together in Europe. Children first experience and learn tenderness from their mothers. Only later do they learn to struggle alongside their fathers. Therefore, the family, and within it the woman, towards whom love and respect are felt and faithfulness is observed, is at least an ideal in European societies. The family helped European societies to overcome conflicts and develop culture. The family provided the initial protection for its members, and they absorbed the foundations of culture into the family.

At the opposite pole from family love, European societies are accompanied by the attempts of some ideologies to appropriate reason. Most recently, communism claimed that it is the only scientifically organized society. It collapsed like a house of cards before the eyes of the present generations. Especially the societies of the post-communist countries remain skeptical about social conceptions, which ridicule their opponents and claim that they are the final draught of truth. This skepticism is contagious, and prophets have already appeared in the new member countries comparing the rules of the European Union to the rules of the former Eastern Block.

The openness of Europe must also be expressed in the method of refuting these false prophets. If the construction of Europe could rely only on rationality expressed in written directives and unwritten political correctness, it would follow the fate of the rational systems, which have, up to the present, always rebelled against their limits. The heritage of the struggle against communism does not contain only skepticism towards totalitarian systems of thought, but also the experience of ordinary human solidarity. It posits the untenability of life as a lie. It contains the liberating force of the free word. It contains the growth of the strength of civil society over the strength of the totalitarian bureaucratic apparatus. The nations of the former Eastern Block bring all this to the treasury of the European Union.

A transcendental whiff blows on the European Union, when it considers the present and future position of religion. Europe without Christianity would not be Europe, and there would be no discussion of its spiritual and cultural dimensions. The report is right to mention the tragic experiences connected with the involvement of the Church and religion in various European conflicts. However, it is impossible to forget the importance of religious motivation in the organization of apparently hopeless resistances to injustice, dictatorship and war, or in ordinary, practical human solidarity. Religion provides the final support, especially in periods of crisis. Europe cannot abandon this heritage. The lessons of communism tell us that no public power succeeds in forcing religion into a position not acceptable to it during the given historical period. Perhaps it is pointless here to attempt a close definition of the position of religion and the Church in society. Let us leave that to religion, the Church and society. The report states that economy cannot provide society with a feeling of unity and solidarity. Religion can. A mention of God in the European Constitution would be a step towards changing the Union from a pragmatic organization to a community of destiny.

The European Union extends from the Atlantic to the slopes of the Carpathians, but Romano Prodi's commission speaks of the dimensions of Europe. Let us not forget, then, that Europe reaches as far as another mountain range: the Urals. Whether the European Union will extend further to the east in the near future, or will repair its relations with Bielorus, Ukraine and Russia with other treaties is now of secondary concern. The mission and ambition of the European Union must be the unification of the whole of our continent, if not institutionally, then at least via a coordination of policy. The Union's key partner in the east is Russia, so permanent dialogue with Russia should be virtually an article of the future European Constitution.

Dialogue with Russia should not be merely economic policy dialogue. Russian culture is part of the highest European culture, and European culture sets the standard for Russia. Russia defended Europe against two conquerors, Napoleon and Hitler, and let us not forget that it did so at immense human sacrifice. Russia very often perceives the West as a threat. It is a historic challenge to the European Union to change this Russian perception of the West. At present, Russia sees the approach of NATO bases to its territory as a threat from the West. The European Union should not support the building of NATO bases further east.

Here we are already dealing with the foreign and security policy of the European Union. However loftily we speak about spiritual and cultural values, the fact remains that Europe also built its position in the world thanks to its military power. It cannot do without military power in the future. The world does not respect the weak, who cannot defend themselves. Weapons of mass destruction have changed the nature of military power and Europe is more vulnerable than any other continent. Nevertheless, Europe cannot give up the military defense of its interests. Whether we place the vulnerability of Europe first, or its spiritual and cultural values, the end result is that Europe should not threaten anyone; it cannot apply its interests in an aggressive way. However, there should be no doubt that Europe can defend its interests against aggressors—if necessary, also militarily, even at the price of loss of life. Europeans should be educated to this fact. Slovaks, Germans, Spanish, Swedes and others should be educated to defend Europe, even at the other side of the continent.

During the fall of communism in Central Europe, mass demonstrations of people chanted "Back to Europe!" The Iron Curtain had divided Europe for 40 years, but it could not destroy the European consciousness of its prisoners. Today we are in Europe. Our European consciousness as free citizens will be different from that of the communist period, but it will not be less.

The Russian poet Tutchev wrote, in a well-known verse, that Russia cannot be grasped by reason, it is necessary to believe in Russia. His verse modified to apply to Europe, which includes Russia, would read: "Europe cannot be grasped by reason, but it is also necessary to believe in it."

UTE FREVERT

Does Europe Need a Cultural Identity?
Ten Critical Remarks

1. The starting point is accurately described: After World War II, Europe was destroyed, materially and mentally devastated. The German National Socialists' (and the Italian Fascists') plans for Europe were bankrupt. They left behind a field of ruins and inflicted on every nation wounds whose scars have not healed to this day. The almost immediately ensuing Cold War added new injuries and divided Europe into two hostile halves, each armed to the teeth. With massive American financial assistance and political support, the countries of Western Europe managed to achieve economic and political stability. The economic dimension stood in the foreground: growing affluence and its broad distribution were regarded as the foundation of a viable democracy, and as the best protection against communist adventures.

2. To strengthen Western Europe against the emerging Soviet bloc, the USA pushed for intense cooperation and coordination, including military and economic resources, in order to minimize internal conflicts and solidify resistance against the Eastern bloc. The approach was pragmatic, not ideological. Instead of invoking European values and proclaiming a European identity, the founding fathers of the EU concentrated on the underpinnings and construction of Western Europe's close economic interaction. France's security policy interests and West Germany's desires for political integration furthered the project. Memories of the ruinous consequences of the European political order installed by the Versailles Treaty served as a warning.

3. But the Western Europe of the early postwar years did not consist solely of members and institutions of the European Coal and Steel Community or the EEC. There were also economic associations like the European Free Trade Association, which no one mentions anymore because it did not survive competition with the E(E)C in the mid-term. And there were (and are) European institutions like the Council of Europe, which saw its task as "to achieve a greater unity between its members for the purpose of safeguarding and realizing the ideals and principles which are their common heritage" (Art. 1 of the 1949 charter). The states joining the Council of Europe in 1950 agreed to the Human Rights Convention, which invoked the "common heritage of intellectual goods, political traditions, respect of freedom and authority of law" (*"das gemeinsame Erbe an geistigen Gütern, politischen Überlieferungen, Achtung der Freiheit und Vorherrschaft des Gesetzes"*). Despite this value-based agreement, the Council of Europe remained institutionally weak and politically toothless. It developed most of its energy within the politics of symbols: the blue European flag with its yellow stars is now familiar to everyone. But it did not become ubiquitously visible and present until the moment when the European Union adopted it.

4. Since the 1970s at the latest, it became ever clearer that, in competition with Western European institutions, the E(E)C would be victorious. Precisely its exclusive concern with economic problems enabled it to apply its powers to the shaping of federal political decision-making structures. These are proving to be a stable foundation for integrating and Europeanizing additional areas of politics. All this came about without the necessity of invoking European values and traditions. Even the "Document on European Identity" worked out in 1975 spoke only marginally about a "common heritage;" the focus was on the European Community's "world-political obligations."

5. This has changed dramatically in recent years. Now we hear ever more about the need to define European identity by emphasizing common roots and traditions. Such recourse to one's self is not new; it already experienced a boom in the 1920s among those associated with the numerous magazines and initiatives focused on "Europe."

During and after World War II, various groups struggled for the power to presume to speak ideologically/visionarily for Europe; conservative Catholic proponents of "the West" competed with Socialist protagonists of a "Third Way." Why such thought has now become socially acceptable within the bodies of the EU, which had thus far kept a fastidious distance to it, demands critical appraisal. The authors of the Europe Paper have two lines of argumentation. First, they assert that the initially effective cohesive forces of the pan-European project (anti-Communism, overcoming the results of the war) have since been dissipated. And second, they maintain that the new ambition to transform the European Economic Community into a political community demands strongly value-based, cultural underpinnings.

6. But do these explanations, which are simultaneously meant as justifications, really hold up? Does Europe really face its end if it does not elaborate its "mental and cultural dimension" more clearly? Is the moral-visionary rearmament everyone bandies about really needed? Doubts are in order. Politically, the EU seems to be firmly in the saddle, and no alternatives are in sight. Certainly, the dramatic devastation of World War II is behind us, and the Cold War is now history as well. But many old fears are still around, and populous and economically potent (even if badly listing) Germany still attracts skepticism and distrust. Knowing it is integrated in the time-tested architecture of the EU has a calming effect, especially on its immediate neighbors. Beyond that, the economic attractiveness of the EU is unbroken. Even if the sum to be distributed may shrink in coming years as economic data decline, while the policy of massive extension feeds growing desires, the coordination offices and redistribution funds in Brussels will lose nothing of their sex appeal. This power of attraction, incidentally, inheres in more than just agricultural subsidies; the EU has extended its grasp to other areas, such as, for example, being active in research policy.

7. It is a European tradition and characteristic to undervalue such material and institutional factors of political cohesion. In contrast to the USA, which (so far) is oriented more in terms of pragmatic considerations, Europe always wants everything based on intellectual ideals. The problem is only that the realm of ideas, values, and ideals is generally conflictual. Consensus is hard to reach here; interpretational battles are probable and are more divisive than unifying. The founding fathers of the European Community showed profound understanding of history and sure political instinct when they avoided this minefield, trusting instead to the integrating power of institutions. Now the authors of the Europe Paper are also having a difficult time defining a "European order of culture and values." Although they believe this is of overriding importance in constituting Europe as a "political subject" and in guaranteeing the cohesion of Europeans, they shy away from naming the ingredients of this "common European culture." Nevertheless, they seem to know what the issue is: common "institutions, ideas and expectations, habits and feelings, moods, memories, and prospects." These are brought together and presented; this culture, it is said, is the basis for the feeling that Europe belongs together.

8. This is doubtful. If anything, it is the vision or dream of a "civil society" that unites the various regions of Europe. But visions and dreams are by definition indistinct. There is no agreement on what constitutes a civil society. Not everything touted under its name can be reconciled with democratic societies' promises of freedom and tolerance. In addition, the practices generally identified with a civil society are mostly carried out in small, surveyable spaces. Those seeking forms of active solidarity and self-organization find them primarily locally; even the nation-state is already too big for them, not to mention the level of "Europe." There is no "European civil society" and therefore no political union can be based on it.

9. But what *does* exist are local initiatives transcending borders and bringing Europeans together—city partnerships, for example, and cooperation projects between hospitals, universities, veterans' associations, and youth groups. In these networks, which the EU supports but cannot control, concrete solidarity develops. Here people learn to listen to and talk with each other. Here they discover common orientations, as well as separating memories. Here people can work on strengthening what they have in common and on enduring what divides them. Here a Europe based on living experiences, rather than on a mummified canon of values and ideas, is arising.

10. But this Europe must be, and remain, open; it must not hunker down and isolate itself behind its new borders. It is not clear why Europeans' solidarity should be directed primarily to Europeans. The idea that doctors in Novgorod deserve less support (though they may need it more) than doctors in Krakow is more than dubious. A "Fortress Europe" would serve no one—Europeans no more than non-Europeans. Efforts to define Europe culturally—even if only as a "culture of civil society"—raise suspicions that they foster such a siege mentality. Strengthening external boundaries to create internal cohesion was a trusted means that 19th-century nation-states employed to cement their "identity." Already at that time, this kind of policy endangered the peace and hindered transnational communication. The European Union should not repeat the same mistake.

DANUTA HÜBNER

Solidarity on Trial

Solidarity is a basic value of the Union. It is highlighted in the draft Constitutional Treaty. It appears as one of the fundamental objectives of the Union and again in the preamble to the Charter of Fundamental Rights, as one of the principles on which the Union is built.

Unfortunately the Constitution cannot match the simple Oxford English Dictionary definition of solidarity as 'unity resulting from common interests, feelings, or sympathies.' Does solidarity in this sense exist within the Union or is it simply a fine word that covers up disunity and national interests? And is solidarity, if it did exist between member states, now stretched to the breaking point by enlargement of the Union to ten relatively poorer and more agricultural new member states? Will this solidarity pass the test of the recent enlargement and beyond?

The Europe Paper argues that the "old forces of integration—the desire for peace, the existence of external threats, and the potential for economic growth—lose their effectiveness," and that "the spiritual factor of European integration will inevitably grow in importance as a source of unity and cohesion." This would imply a shift in the European identity paradigm that—in my view—moves from identifying Europe by what unites us towards identifying it by what differentiates us from the rest of the world. I would not feel very comfortable with this change.

Nobody would question that culture contributes to Europe's unity. However, let us not forget that Europe's history contains periods when neighboring cultures did not communicate, as well as periods of strong cultural cohesion, which, unfortunately, did not prevent the outbreak of endless wars between Europeans. While I would agree that cultural and spiritual factors matter greatly, I would insist that economic and political unity, as well as common institutions, are a precondition to sustainable peace in Europe and to Europe's successful response to globalization.

It is also worth pointing out that the old forces are still significant. While we can accept the fact that peace between the European nations is assured and that they have ceased to be a potent force for further integration, they remain fundamental values for all Europeans. Indeed when we look around the troubled world, we should be careful about assuming anything about peace in Europe. We need to keep working at ensuring that the conditions for peace are guaranteed in the long-term future. I would also qualify the external threats to peace as being more dangerous than those that existed before 1990.

I think we should also point out that the performance of the economy is a fundamental part of the integration process. It is difficult to imagine solidarity in the Union growing stronger in the face of a serious economic downturn. Indeed, our experience of recent years shows us that slow economic growth in Europe has already led to some real decline in the feeling of solidarity and may be a contributing factor in reducing public support for integration in the Union. Therefore, the link between economic performance and solidarity matters. One should, however, ask the question whether this is really a result of poor economic growth or has more to do with a change in European society.

I would attribute this worrisome decline in solidarity—even though it is a characteristic of European society in general—to three factors: the rise of individualism, the strain of accelerating social change, and poor economic performance.

Yet we nonetheless have a stronger basis for reinforcing solidarity in the Union than we sometimes think. The twenty-five member states share fundamental values as well as interests, not to mention their history. Even in their '*Weltanschauungen*' they seem remarkably similar when viewed from outside. We Europeans often talk about the contrast between the liberal, individualistic, private sector-orientated British and Irish, as opposed to the statist tendencies of the French and the Germans, with their national championships and extensive social security systems. But looked at from America, Asia or Africa, these differences are not at all obvious. In spite of Donald Rumsfeld's remarks, Europe is definitely seen from outside as a whole, and clearly distinct from the economic and social systems prevalent in other parts of the world.

From outside, Europe is thought to be 'more social' and 'more compassionate' than many other societies. This is part of the 'common European cultural space' the paper talks about. Our challenge is to combine this with efficiency in the global economy. We must avoid descending into a totally individualistic, egoistic society. I disagree with Margaret Thatcher, who is supposed to have said that 'society' as a concept did not exist, but we must avoid the trap of developing into a society wherein individual merit and risk-taking are stifled and enterprises suffocated.

I want to challenge the view that solidarity has been put at risk by the enlargement of the Union to the countries of Central and Eastern Europe. I would suggest that this is in fact not the case and that the values and interests of the new member states coincide in most ways with those of the EU-15. However, it is certainly true that the enlargement has fundamentally changed the Union and given rise to new policy concerns and some new problems. The new member states in Central and Eastern Europe are deeply embedded in the economic, social and cultural development of our Continent. The ties that bind us together were challenged by forty years of Soviet domination, but this has not fundamentally changed the European character of these European states.

My country, Poland, has always had deep cultural ties to the other European countries, especially to France. We have participated in all the major developments in European film culture, as well as in music and literature. In sports, the German national football team before the First World War consisted entirely of players with Polish names. But, above all, there is a sentiment among Poles, but also among Hungarians, Czechs and others, that they are Europeans in a very deep sense. This is what the Oxford Dictionary calls 'unity resulting from feelings and sympathies.'

Solidarity, in the sense of unity resulting from common interests, also clearly exists within the Union, both the EU-15 and the enlarged Union. This is really demonstrated by the very few policy issues on which there is disunity. The disunity over the Iraq question disguises the fact that member state foreign ministers agree on almost all the foreign affairs dossiers that arrive on their desks. Disagreements on the question of the community patent disguise the fact that the internal market has never been contested by any member state, new or old.

The enlargement process itself is also manifestly a symbol of European social, civic and cultural unity. The fact that there was much debate over the enlargement, as well as some dispute, should not be allowed to detract from the fact that both the old member states and the new were convinced that they had an obligation to rebuild the Continent after 40 years of division. The enlargement is an expression of just those cultural and spiritual dimensions that Professors Biedenkopf and Michalski discuss in their paper.

But how do we deal with the questions that the two authors raise at the end of their paper? Europe is no longer a purely Jewish/Christian and white continent. Will our citizens whose origin is on another continent and whose religion is Hindu or Islam, Sikh or Buddhist, be able to identify with these 'European' values, with European culture? Will they be able to feel European, as the Poles or the Czechs have always felt? This question applies equally to the enlargement with Turkey. Is European integration about respecting someone's values? Is it about sharing them or about contributing to them, or about being capable of contributing to them constantly?

These are difficult questions. They are particularly difficult if we see culture as a cement for the future of Europe. I think all countries started off believing that their migrants could be assimilated in the same way that Polish migrants were assimilated into the Ruhr region in the nineteenth century. That this has not happened, at least on a large scale, is not to say that it cannot happen. Look at the growing number of prominent Turkish-origin citizens in Germany. Or at how many second generation Indian and Pakistani Britons one now sees in business suits and with computers, flying everywhere in the world. But we have to admit that these are still the exceptions rather than the rule. Once again, I am sure that solidarity must play a role in this integration process. Many of our immigrant groups find themselves on the edge of our societies. They are flung back into their own communities by the impossibility of social and economic integration with mainstream society. The constant threat of terrorism has made this isolation even more dramatic for Islamic populations.

These problems must be addressed if we are going to ensure that we have a Union of values with 'unity resulting from feelings and sympathies.'

Europe is different. Europe is a continent we all love, with values that we all admire. But we cannot rest there. The spiritual and cultural dimension of Europe will not survive neglect. It requires continual care and development if it is going to be the element that drives forward integration in Europe.

LECH KACZYNSKI

Europe—Still Divided

Almost a quarter of a century has passed since Tadeusz Mazowiecki's famous article "The other face of Europe." In evaluating the significance of the appointment of Karol Woytyla to the throne of St.
Peter's, Mazowiecki, who went on to become the first president of
independent Poland, reminded us that aside from the happy, western
part of the continent, there is also a central and central eastern part,
which, while belonging to the same historical–cultural community,
finds itself in a completely different situation. It was necessary to
deliver this reminder, because the community which Mazowiecki
was appealing to had at that time been forgotten. Perhaps it would be
better to say that it had been disregarded, and that the condition of
slavery had, basically, been accepted. This meant the same thing as
the denial of the historical community, and also, in an ethical sense,
of the mutual belonging of citizens in both parts of Europe, and the
resulting solidarity. Now it is said that this is just how it was at the
end of the 1970s, that it was a long time ago, and that today everything is completely different: the other Europe now belongs to the
Union, or soon will, so the division has been overcome, and with it
the political, cultural and moral problem. This viewpoint has many
supporters. I will make no song and dance about the fact that I am
not one of them, which of course does not mean that I would under-
estimate the significance of what occurred in 2004. If I nonetheless
raise doubts, these are ones born out of the developments of the 1990s
and of recent times, the analysis of which obliges me to draw a regret-
table conclusion: namely, that it is unlikely that in the future my

country, and also others in "the other Europe," will be participatory in the full extent of European solidarity.

The attitude taken by Western Europeans from after World War II until 1989, namely to take the division of Europe for granted and to write off the other half, can be viewed as the result of a process of normalization in social consciousness—as the rationalization of a decision whose effect, once taken, became more irreversible the more any alternative appeared risky and uncertain. This attitude still marks the perception of, and dealings with, the former "eastern Europe" fifteen years after the fall of the Iron Curtain. It should be changed immediately, above all with regard to those in the region who—like most of Europe—fell victim to German Nazism, and who were only allowed to celebrate their liberation fifty years later.

Analogies between the eastern enlargement and the Marshall Plan, which benefited Germany in particular, are popular. This parallel, however, is completely misleading, because our relations to the Union are founded upon an unequal principle: the advantages for the Union member-states are greater than those for Poland. Most disturbing is not merely the fact that the membership process was drawn out longer than that of Greece or Spain; it is much more the fact of what we have been confronted with *since* becoming members of the Union. In order to present the reasons for this disturbance, allow me to make one or two observations about the history of the European Union and the European Economic Community (EEC) from our perspective.

The formation of the EEC was the result of the experiences of the First and Second World Wars, and was at the same time an alliance against Communism. The idea of a union of Europe was not new; now, however, there was the impetus to make it a historical fact. This was a union founded upon the recognition of the existence, equality, and sovereignty of the nation-states, upon the recognition of democracy as a fundamental precondition for the union's legitimacy, and not least of all, upon the recognition that democracy itself has deeper foundations, namely values, that grew out of Christianity and its lessons about the primacy and worth of the human being.

The EEC and its predecessor organizations were the work of Christian Democrats, a political formation that attempted to combine elements of conservatism, liberalism, and socialism, whereby democracy was the only one to refer directly to the worth of the human being. The equality of states thus meant the equality of societies, and by extension, of peoples and individuals. With the recognition of national particularities came the recognition that individuals are able to realize their rights only in the realm of their own cultural and historical belonging. Furthermore, it was recognized that the European community is a community of communities, but that a political community of all Europeans which bypasses the national communities is a postulate referring to a very distant and indefinite future, entertained by only a few.

This construction of the EEC led to the recognition of the principle of solidarity as the basic condition for the organizational and financial functioning of the community, and for its underlying values. Solidarity meant an aspiration not only for formal equality (one state, one vote), but also for real equality; in other words, the levelling of the economic standard of the European states, as well as that of individual regions within those states. It also meant the rejection of hegemony. For this reason, it is possible to say that the conception of the EEC offered a rebuttal to the classical political principle of the balance of power, since this was founded on the controlled tension between states.

When looking at the history of the EEC and the Union, it must not be forgotten that their formation, as well as the greater part of their existence, has been marked, on one hand, by heavy pressure from the east and simultaneous protection from America, and, on the other, by an exclusivity that was only really corrected in 1985, when 50 million Spaniards and Portuguese were admitted to the Union. The policies of de Gaulle must also not be forgotten: these represented an attempt to return to classical hegemonic politics within the Community, and simultaneously to pit the Community against the US.

Although in the course of time the constructivist tendency grew within the Union, the founding ideas endured. This changed significantly with the enlargement, and with the parallel suggestion of providing the Union with a constitution. The Nice Treaty, however, preserved at least several elements of the original conception. The principle of unanimity had indeed been limited; it, however, raised the value of small- and medium-sized countries, thereby providing the newly admitted states from the "other Europe" a relatively good starting position. The European Constitution, as it concerned these states, signified a general change of course with regard both to its text and its context.

Let's begin with the preamble. There were two reasons why we demanded that the Christian traditions in these countries be borne in mind. First, we wanted the truth to be respected, because we knew from our experience—the experience of communism, and also post-communism—what it meant to live in a system wherein it was disregarded. Second, we saw in this element of the preamble a point of connection to the founding idea of the European Union, one that is important to us. And last, because of the inclusion of the Christian tradition in the preamble, we thought that each state in which Christianity was still alive (of which Poland is one) would be granted a certain respect. We feared anti-Christian censorship. And when this occurs in a Constitution, censorship has its foot in the door.

Recent experiences have confirmed this. Now, the issue has ceased to become one of censorship, and become one of the penalization of statements underpinned by faith, one of discrimination against Catholics. Nothing else lies behind the resignation of Commissioner Buttiglione and the charges brought against a Swedish pastor.

We see another, equally difficult, problem: the radical restriction of the sovereignty of nation-states, on one hand by the European constitution, to which the national constitutions are subordinated, and on the other by the enormous extent of the legislation to be implemented by the Union, rather than the nation-states. In actual fact, we are dealing with two problems: first, the restriction of the democratic principle that only representative bodies have legislative authority, and, second, the transfer of national sovereignty from the smaller and weaker states to the more powerful.

This situation is rendered more acute by further factors: the inexperience of the newly-admitted states in the political arena of the Union; the discourteous language used to address them; the German–French anti-Americanism and its lack of understanding for the new member-states' natural desire to seek the support of the US, the only power to promise them protection from Russian claims. Privileges for the territory of the former GDR, which Germany is loathe to give up, complete the picture.

A lack of regard for history is reflected here, along with the inseparable issue of guilt for World War II and its consequences. Privileges are received by a country directly involved in the fifty-year subjugation of Central and Central Eastern Europe, and which incurred guilt for monstrous crimes there. In fact, what we observe here is a hierarchy of nations, and also of individuals according to their national affiliation, a hierarchy ultimately based on power.

Economic issues also ought not to be overlooked. The future constitution anticipates a harmonization of economic policy. For the time being, at least, it is still a vaguely intimated perspective. It is, however, one which has already been interpreted in a practical way in the form of the demand that new member-states raise their taxes— in other words, subordinate their own economic interests to those of the stronger partners.

Lastly, there is the mystifying phenomenon whereby the stronger states appeal permanently to Europe and to European belonging, but forget all forms of solidarity as soon as the issue becomes one of budgeting. If we want to strengthen the institutions of the Union and give it the status of a proto-nation-state, then the means the Union has at its disposal (in other words, the budget) must be raised. The reality, however, it is precisely the reverse. As one might expect, it is reflected in the immediate expression of solidarity in the form of help for economically weaker states and regions.

The most obvious tendency with regard to expenditures is for national regulation to be renounced in favor of the effort towards transnational uniformity. I have already mentioned the transfer of sovereignty from weaker to stronger states. I must add here that this is expected to take place at a low price. The union will not hear of support for the new member-states along the lines of that once received by Ireland, Greece, Spain, or southern Italy. This can hardly be judged to be an expression of solidarity.

If one looks at what is going on in the Union today, there can be no doubt that it is all about the interests of the larger and economically more powerful European states, who wish to construct a Union that secures for them a stronger position in the world than corresponds to their potential, and above all, their readiness to pull their own weight. There is no reason why we should accept this, or even go along with this type of politics—least of all Poland, which has every right to entertain greater ambitions.

Furthermore, we are not ready to take on the various challenges facing us that have to do with Germany's leading role. If the political correctness that today supersedes Christianity as the basic value system takes on an anti-Christian, and in particular an anti-Catholic, character—something directed especially at Poland—then we will refuse to accept this as well. The same goes for the new version of history that the Euro-enthusiasts would like to create, a history in which victims and executioners no longer exist.

Therefore, as decided supporters of a Union which lays the foundations for a lasting solidarity of European states, we are unable to declare ourselves in agreement with a constitution that undermines the foundations for such solidarity, and contains elements that in essence perpetuate the division of Europe. We demand nothing more than that which in part has already been granted to others and has united Europe, namely solidarity.

Translated from the German by Simon Garnett

IRA KATZNELSON

Reflections on Solidarity

The central concept in the Europe Paper is 'solidarity,' with a focus on values that might integrate a diverse, often fractious, European continent. I believe the concept to be more inherently complex than the essay signifies, so it is about this intricacy and density that I wish to comment. For when we speak about solidarity, its content is not self-evident. Nor are the values on which it stands. Indeed, I have constructed a short-list of attractive normative possibilities of meaning for the term. Each, we will quickly see, is morally appealing. Yet each possesses internal contradictions, and, to some extent, has an uneasy relationship to the others.

Let me explain what I mean. One basis of solidarity would be a shared commitment to liberty. A second might be a shared commitment to certain moral values—say about the worth of the human person. A third might be solidarity with respect to the way in which governments act to create conditions in which citizenship becomes meaningful by helping to secure a threshold of social and economic equality. This is solidarity based on common social citizenship. Fourth, we could mean by solidarity collective understandings of how the polity—whether a nation-state or a semi-formal polity like the European Union—constructs a common position that evokes solidarity amongst elites and citizens with respect to other polities in the international arena.

Each one of these potential arenas of potential solidarity is internally contested. There is, quite obviously, no single correct or uncontroversial basis for defining the dimension of liberty. Issues concerning whose liberty, what liberty, and which individuals get to be within the zone of liberty—including issues of membership, immigration, and minority status like that of the Roma in Europe and African Americans in the United States—continue to be subjects of robust dispute.

The Western liberal tradition, which has much to say about such values as consent, toleration, political representation, and basic rights, has nothing inherent to say about who gets to be a liberal citizen and how access to liberty is to be secured by all. If this is to be the basis of Europe's solidarity, clearly much remains to be done to clarify relevant values, policies, and circumstances. Perhaps no issue will challenge Europe more with regard to this zone of solidarity than that of potential Turkish admission to the EU.

Likewise, there are deeply conflicted understandings about the moral and ethical bases of respect for the individual person. Although Europe, in the main, is the globe's most secularly oriented region, the meaning of such respect remains contested—at times, as in recent disputes concerning homosexuality and membership in the European Commission, in religious terms. We see these kinds of disputes about the meaning of life, family, and sexuality more directly in the American polity, because there is a part of my country's political discourse that is shamelessly religious. I say shamelessly, because it is meant to mobilize votes through religious commitments. But such issues do not go away, even when politicians avoid the kind of talk that appeals to evangelical Protestants or traditional Catholics in the United States. The question of what the normative basis of respect for the person, for the group, and for life—to use that charged word—should be essentially contested, not just in the United States, but in every single country I know in Europe.

Equally, the dimension of solidarity concerned with the role of government in creating meaningful and just social citizenship is not an area where agreement, let along consensus, comes naturally. In very broad terms, there is talk of a European social model, but every party system and every parliamentary arena is rife with disagreement about the composition of this model. So, too, is solidarity based on foreign policy. Secretary Rumsfeld's binary distinction between 'old' and 'new' Europe may have been tendentious and ill-intentioned, but he accurately identified a profound lack of cohesion on the continent with regard to the policies of the United States and the role of multilateral institutions.

The very concept of solidarity, in short, is internally heterogeneous, conflictual and not simply additive. The maximization of goods in one dimension or arena of solidarity may, depending on the circumstances, create problems for the maximization of moral and other goods at other levels that can also provide the basis for solidarity. Conflict within zones and conflict across zones implies that, unavoidably and perpetually, there are choices to be made, not just about whether to promote a common—say European or American or Western—solidarity, but about the kind of solidarity we wish to have.

Solidarity is a conception composed of layers, each of which is something like a continuous variable, to use a social science term. Each dimension—whether it concerns liberty, the human person, social justice, or collective international policy—can possess more or less specific, often controversial, values; these dimensions combine and recombine in different ways at different moments as products of a political process. Decent democratic politics directly confronts choices about these dimensions of solidarity.

None of the 'goods' that define solidarity in each dimension, moreover, are ever possessed equally by all citizens, or potential citizens. There is with respect to each of these aspects, as an empirical matter (both in the United States and in Europe), a great deal of inequality. Not every citizen enjoys freedom equally; not every life is valued equally; not every citizen enjoys social justice equally; not every client group gains from an active government; not every citizen can influence or shape foreign policy. Hierarchies of power are steep. At a minimum, they challenge each of solidarity's bases. Sometimes, they are so exorbitant that they mock the concept itself, revealing it, at times, to be a specious or utopian conceit.

Solidarity, moreover, has to be judged not as a good 'a priori,' but a good in terms of its capacity to deal with crisis and to grapple with human diversity. The very conception of solidarity as a normative and institutional basis for organizing social reality, the very character of solidarity, implies a capacity to perform positive tasks. We would not wish to worry about solidarity unless we thought its absence would make it harder to perform those valued tasks.

We need to judge solidarity not simply in the abstract, but in terms of the particular mix or configuration or constellation of elements that compose it, and in terms of its ability to deal, first of all, with deep potential economic, social, political, or geopolitical crises which come at some point for all of us, and, secondly, with the most remarkable feature of Western modernity: its demographic, cultural, social and geographic diversity. If we cannot deal with diversity, if solidarity cripples diversity, then it will fail. If solidarity is merely a cover for good times but cannot help us get through hard times, it is not much of a model or ideal for social integration.

Let us not assume that the more solidarity the better. But all depends on what kind. The last century offers us many examples of strong solidarities that were not just ugly, but far worse. We also know from sociological literature that social solidarity may be the result of what the network analyst, Mark Granovetter, calls "the strength of weak ties." It is possible to build durable social structures on the basis of ties which are not very tightly bound, but which, indeed, are weaker than a threshold level often looked to when we talk about high levels of solidarity.

Let me give an example from the history of the American trade union movement: in the 1930s, a period of massive growth in membership for mass production unions in the United States, the working class population in those factories was remarkably heterogeneous. How did Polish immigrants, Irish immigrants, Jewish immigrants, German immigrants, and black immigrants from the South actually fashion union solidarity? Traditional Marxist analysis might say "of course they'd be solidaristic, they are members of the working class," but it is not so simple to form a solidaristic trade union in the face of such cultural diversity. A good argument can be made that the ethnic and religious groups who composed this union working class of the 1930s brought with them experiences of local trust. Robust local ties facilitated the construction of paradoxically 'weak' yet 'strong' links among these workers. Thus, as an example, Polish neighborhood solidarity organizations taught people practices of trust that they then transferred across ethnic, religious and racial lines in workplace settings. The unions were built on weak ties layered on top of strong ties.

We thus need to think harder about the nature of networks that connect people, both elites and masses, in different social groups and different social classes to each other in common public spheres. We need to think about those networks as consisting not only of one valence or one level, but also of heterogeneous linkages in terms of varieties of strength and weakness. Finally, we have to think about solidarity as a boundary condition. If we speak of European solidarity or American solidarity or human solidarity, each site of solidarity implies a set of boundaries—between people and among normative and institutional positions. This is never a single list of values. Rather, solidarity is composed as a perpetually contested set of configurations combining values and institutions in distinct constellations.

From this perspective, the European Union and the terms of its solidarity are so very important, from an American point of view. We have an enormous stake in the success of Europe in these terms. Only within a framework that goes beyond the traditional European nation-states is it possible to imagine the development of this kind of thick and thin, pluralistically contested, democratic form of solidarity. Only that kind of solidarity can confront crisis when it comes or sensitively grapple with the various types of human diversity.

These issues of solidarity challenge both Europe and the United States. Despite all our differences, we face broadly common problems about how to think about the relationship between state and citizen, between state and economy, between the state and other states, and especially, about questions of membership. In addition to identifying our differences, I hope we can also identify broadly common challenges to our very similar polities in terms of their deepest and best commitments: to toleration, to consent, to political representation and the like.

We also need to talk about Europe and America in more subtle and richer relational, rather than simply comparative, terms. Think of the period that spans the Second World War and the first decade after. It is impossible to understand the history of European integration at that time without understanding that at the end of the Second World War only the American New Deal stood as a large-scale model of a polity that had managed the crises of capitalist collapse and the mass appeal of totalitarian regimes. Only the New Deal surmounted these challenges. This had a profound influence in the making of postwar Europe. Surely there is more continuity between post-Second World War European social democracy and the left-of-center part of the American New Deal than there was continuity between pre-War and post-War social democracy in Europe.

In short, we cannot compose the history of the post-War years unless we write it relationally. We cannot record the history of the Cold War unless we write it in relation, one nation to the other. Today, whatever is going to happen with respect to European integration will, yet again, be deeply affected by the quality and character of the relationship with the United States—as a foil, as a partner, or as another polity broadly working out the complexity of the meaning of solidarity under common difficult and also democratic conditions. I thus very much hope—not simply for the sake of Europe, but for the sake of the United States—that the conversation that takes place in Europe about values and integration and solidarity will overlap with similar conversations under way inside the American polity.

The last thing I want to observe is this: I was very much informed by the Europe Paper, but I confess to a certain skepticism about the amount of weight it places on the value dimension itself because, as I have noted, the values at issue in the quest for solidarity are always internally heterogeneous and contested. I would speak in a sober way about the threshold conditions for solidarity on the understanding, as the paper underscores so well, that Europe is a project that unfolds, and that the central challenge of European solidarity is therefore that of creating boundary conditions within which that unfolding can take place productively.

IVAN KRASTEV

Europe's Solidarity Deficit

What once upon a time was the "unification of Europe" has turned into the enlargement of the EU. But it is precisely because the enlargement of the European Union is no longer the unification of Europe that Brussels faces a major problem—a problem that is more profound than the democracy deficit: the solidarity deficit.

In 1992 the President of the European Commission, Jacque Delors, called for "a soul of Europe," arguing that if Brussels wasn't able to inject a spiritual dimension into the EU, it would fail to command the allegiance of its citizens. Delors's words were often quoted, but never taken seriously. The EU of today is a triumph of political constructivism.

In the context of this over-powerful institutionalist perspective on the future, the conclusions of the Reflection Group on the Spiritual and Cultural Dimension of Europe are both thoughtful and timelier than ever. They bring back the problem of Europe's soul, not as an intellectual, but as an urgent, political issue. And this takes place in a political context where any mention of the cultural foundations of the EU is perceived as a veiled criticism of Turkey's membership in the Union.

In the view of the Reflection Group, "political union needs political cohesion, a politically grounded solidarity and common interests." In this view, the existing factors of cohesion are losing their relative significance. The common experience of WWII, the common external threat (the Soviet Union), and the economic growth and promise of affluence as community-forming goals are losing their effectiveness. Europe needs cultural foundations. Only culture can compen-

sate for the increasingly obvious lack of solidarity in Europe—a lack
of solidarity not only on an institutional, but also on an individual,
level. In the words of the Europe Paper: "when individual solidarity
is not there, institutionally based solidarity is not enough to bring a
polity into being." The mobilization of European solidarity is defined
as *the* important long-term task of European politics.

My own reflections on the state of European project shares a
similar concern. A deficiency of solidarity is what really should be
bothering anybody who believes that the EU is something more than
a common market or a common security space. But while the group's
reflections are focused on the decline of solidarity in the the "old
Europe," what really worries me is the lack of solidarity in the "new
Europe." This deficit of individual solidarity could be observed both
on the level of one's own society, and even more on the level of
Europe as a whole. The truth is that the new EU members suffered
an even more profound lack of solidarity, both inside their own societies and with respect to Europe, than did Western Europeans. In a
way similar to Western Europe, Eastern European societies have lost
the three sources of their "Solidarity moment," namely the communist
state they opposed, the economy of deficit that brought them together
on a day-to-day basis, and the sense of national dignity they preserved against the internationalist orthodoxy of official Marxism. It
does not require special research to conclude that the societies that
gave birth to "Solidarity" are lacking solidarity.

The intuition of the Reflection Group is that one of the sources
for solidarity-building in Europe could be a re-consideration of the
role of religions (in plural) within the European project. Though
never explicitly stated, it is obvious that the group does not believe
the EU can succeed as a secularist project. In this respect there are
striking parallels between some of the arguments presented in the
Europe Paper and the discussions in Polish leftist oppositional cir-
cles somewhere around 1976–1980. Therefore, it might be a good
idea for some of the proponents of EU integration to re-read Mich-
nik's book, "The Church and the Left," written exactly in 1976.

The conclusions of the Reflection Group recommend a new dialogue and *rapprochement* between the Left and different religions in
Europe. This is a very important message, but it should be read with
an understanding of the different contexts. For someone like me,

coming from a country where the Orthodox Church failed to reestablish solidarity in the society and where its basic objective is to use the power of the state to preserve its dominant role, the prospects for real dialogue are not extremely promising. But, in other parts of Europe, this could be exactly what is needed.

What is at stake is a pan-European *rapprochement* between religions (primarily Catholicism and Islam) and the Left. But could this rapprochement be the framework for re-negotiating the soul of Europe?

In my view such a dialogue is not going to be an easy one. On one hand, the European Left is scared by the rise of the role of religion in the U.S., and it is the secular character of the European project that constitutes the very definition of the new European identity. On the other hand, the rise of Islam will reactivate the public presence of the Christian Churches and strengthen fundamentalist trends in the Catholic Church. This is the worst-case scenario. But this is not the only possible scenario, and we should be grateful to the Reflection Group for the opportunity to discuss more than merely one.

CLAUS LEGGEWIE

Turkey's EU Membership as a Litmus Test of European Self-Confidence

What sets the Europe Paper of the Reflection Group apart from many declarations on Europe is its clear rejection of an essentialist concept of culture—such as, for example, a (Christian) guiding culture—as the possible basis for both a collective establishment of identity and for practical integration policies. Europe is not some kind of cultural essence, but an open historical process and Europe's identity has always been defined in de-centered and extra-territorial terms. If the religious factor is to be taken into account, then it should be so, *not* by limiting and binding Europe to a Christian tradition (again understood as an essentialist one), but by assimilation of and reflection on the foundation of religious peace in a secular Europe, as well as by that inclusive principle of religious freedom that the American constitution today offers on a global level.

It should also be emphasized (even if in fact it should be taken as self-evident) that the Europe Paper does not define itself against an "other" called Islam. The internal diversity of the worldwide Muslim community is not ignored, nor is the fact that, thanks to immigration, Muslims have long been living in Europe, mostly as secularized new European citizens.

These preliminary remarks can be considered with reference to the question that, despite the eastward expansion of the European Union, dominated the debate on (European) integration: the accession of Turkey. In terms of policy deliberation, it is not at all necessary to pre-empt the results of the EU Commission's review and the (more or less) democratic decision-making processes of the states of the European Union here in order to justify a position for or against.

Instead, perspectives on identity and integration policy will be summed up, bearing in mind the determination of the "finality of Europe." The debate on Turkey was extremely helpful and stimulating in this respect.

Turkey has been knocking at the door of the European Community for more than forty years. At first, questions of European identity were not much of an issue. "Turkey is part of Europe. That is the deepest meaning of this process: it is, in the form most appropriate to our times, the confirmation of a truth, which is more than the abbreviated expression of a geographical statement or a historical observation, valid for a few centuries," observed the President of the European Economic Community, Walter Hallstein (CDU), on the occasion of the Agreement of Association between the EEC and Turkey on September 12, 1963. He gave a very favorable assessment of Turkey's convergence with Europe since Kemal Atatürk: "There has been nothing comparable in the history of the influence of European culture and politics, indeed we feel here an essential relationship with the most modern events in Europe... What, therefore, is more natural, than for there to be an identity between Europe... and Turkey in their actions and reactions: military, political and economic."

How different is the optimism of the "Mr Europe" of those days, who foresaw Turkey as "one day" becoming a full member, from the rejection pronounced by today's "Monsieur l'Europe," the President of the European Union Convention, Valéry Giscard d'Estaing, who dogmatically declared that Turkey was "no part of Europe" and its entry would effectively mean the end of the European Union! The reasons for that are due in part to the internal political development of Turkey, to its shortcomings with respect to democracy, economic development and the rule of law, but even more to the reservations of the old members of the Union that have been growing since 1963.

The irony of the history of the last 40 years is that the European Economic Community has meanwhile developed into a political union, while Turkey has become a more strongly Islamic republic, resulting in a quite different context from 1963. Will the end of the story, then, be that an EU now plagued by doubts about identity will refuse entry to a Turkey governed by moderate Islamists, even though the conditions set are being better fulfilled today than ever before? And will the European Union just at this moment, when Turkish society and

government are moving ahead with the political transformation
demanded of them, call off the experiment in democratization, without being able to offer a tangible alternative below the level of full
membership?

The debate on Turkey's EU membership, to which both supporters and opponents have contributed serious arguments, comes in two
parts: one strand documents the process of European self-discovery,
oriented to principles and mainly relating to the old members, establishing their identity by contrast to Turkey—as was done in the past
by contrast to the "Orient." In this debate we can discern five concepts
of identity (and the corresponding objections):

- Europe as a *geographical space* with fixed natural boundaries
  (against which may be set the a priori *eccentric* identity of
  Europe and its great extra-territorial influence);
- Europe as a historically shaped *community with a common mem-
  ory and destiny* (devalued by a *waning historical conscious-
  ness*);
- Europe as heir to the *Christian West* (contradicted by rapid *de-
  Christianisation* and growing *religious pluralism*);
- Europe as a *capitalist market community* with welfare state
  elements (questionable because of *neoliberal globalization*);
- Europe as bulwark of *democracy and human rights* (which as
  universal values and norms cannot be regionally restricted).

The other strand of the debate is concerned, as opposed to the background of the last two assumptions, with the more "technical" question of whether, and when, Turkey fulfils the criteria that the EU
Commission and heads of government laid down at the EU summit
in Copenhagen in December of 2002. In addition to economic performance, they measure, above all, the success of democratization
and actual progress in human, civil and minority rights.

What is taking place under these very precise conditions is the
breathtaking experiment of a policy of social and political change in
a sovereign state (*Drittstaat*) implemented from outside and likewise
evaluated externally. It is an experiment that has attracted too little
attention. Following the program of forced Westernization that the
Turkish Republic has already been following since 1923, this makes
the Turkey's current accession process one of the most exciting democratization projects in modern history, comparable in its radicalism to

the modernization of Japan that began in the 19ᵗʰ century. It is also a good example of the fact that a human rights policy in international relations is no longer mere rhetoric, but produces conclusive, possibly irreversible, results. With reference to the Reflection Group's Europe Paper, it is not a question of how much Turkey Europe can bear (or the other way round). It is, rather, a question of the ability of the Old World to enforce the option of civil democratization in a foreseeable situation of intensified conflict in the geopolitically delicate region of the "Greater Middle East."

The qualification of a country for membership is judged *first* by the extent to which democracy as a way of life has been achieved, which does not simply mean regular democratic elections, but also an independent judiciary, a fair penal system, respect for the cultural rights of ethnic and religious minorities as well as basic and civil rights in general and, not least of all, civilian control of the military. This allows for some kind of measurement as to how long the path to a liberal and pluralist democracy actually still is in Turkey.

At the same time, however, it cannot simply be assumed, that democratization will proceed everywhere in accordance with the same pattern. Rather, it will display cultural undertones and refinements, which must be respected. Democratization after 1945 was everywhere linked to the model character of Western societies and to market liberalization. The specific dialectic of the Turkish path is that democratization went along with, and was accelerated by, a movement of re-Islamization, and so was ultimately based on a desire for religious freedom and cultural autonomy. That in turn allows one to understand the strain that such a transformation brings with it for a secular, unitary republic like Turkey that deliberately disregards such particularisms.

A *second* criterion is the economic strength of a society, and this currently puts Turkey at the level of a not particularly stable, if fast developing, country. But this gap also holds true, by and large, for other aspiring members, and the related risks are already present. This is thanks to associations through the customs unions as well as to the multitude of transnational relations between companies in Turkey itself and in the "diaspora" of Germany and other EU states that are simultaneously sources of economic dynamism and integration. It must not be forgotten that a European Union with the goal of being a social union, with approximately equal living standards throughout its territory, faces greater pressures of expectation and adaptation than a more loosely structured free trade area.

The *third* security policy criterion is often articulated in the current debate in terms of the provocative question of whether the EU wants to find itself sharing a border with Iraq. This is, first of all, an allusion to the Kurdish question, which is seen as the principal internal political problem standing in the way of Turkey's desire for membership, but it also alludes to the geopolitical dynamic in the whole Near and Middle East, where the reduced strategic significance of Turkey as a NATO member since 1990 should also be taken into account. Against this background, the EU must ask itself whether it would be better in the long-term to turn the explosive potential of "North Iraq" into an internal matter, or to try to keep it at arm's length and continue to delegate the problem to the U.S. or medium-sized regional powers.

This alternative once again poses the question of the "old" and "new" Europe, but in a different way: do we want a "Fortress Europe," keeping its distance both from the oriental trouble spots and also from the U.S., deepening its association (rather than extending it) to create a European federal state with a more or less "europhile" periphery? Or do we want an expanded EU, aiming at a capability for worldwide intervention, which could pursue quasi-imperial policies, explicitly competing with the U.S., but with more benevolent goals than the latter? Each alternative's policy toward Turkey, but also toward Syria and Iran, would be substantially different. It poses a difficult choice, but a choice that must be made.

For those who want to "deepen" Europe, then, the relative poverty of Turkey, the future size of its population, the Anatolian coloring of its democracy, the presumed otherness of Islam and, not least of all, potential conflicts with its neighbors will all be cause for alarm. Those, on the other hand, who would like to expand the Union will place their trust in the potential of the developing Turkish economy, in the great number of new (and young) EU citizens, in Islamic variants of democracy, in the building of bridges to Central Asia and the Gulf, and, not least of all, in the prospect of a pacification of the whole region.

Translated from the German by Martin Chalmers

ULRIKE LUNACEK

European and Global Solidarity

Ad 2) The Union has been enormously successful. It established durable bonds, which made a European civil war virtually impossible. The Union established a zone of peace founded on freedom, the rule of law, and social justice.

While this might be true, in the era of globalization we cannot disregard the role that the European Union plays in the world. Armed conflict no longer exists within the EU, yet this is not at all true beyond its borders. The EU must bear a measure of responsibility for what occurs in other parts of the world based on its involvement in the global economy and also due to the colonial past of many of its member states.

In economic contexts, measured by the volume of foreign trade or achievements in the area of developmental work, the EU has long been a global player. It is the greatest contributor to developmental aid and, in recent years, has been willing to eliminate duties for imports from the poorest nations, with no limitation as to amount, in the framework of the "everything but arms" initiative (weapons are excluded, and interim regulations are in effect for bananas, sugar, and rice).

In the global context, for example in negotiations in the context of the UNO, the EU is often equated with civil, or human and minority rights that still meet with protest elsewhere. These include, to name but a few, fair access to the justice system, individual freedoms, women's rights, an independent media, environmental protection, and equal rights and anti-discrimination measures protecting people from discrimination on the basis of ethnic origins or sexual orientation.

It is quite a different picture with negotiations at the World Trade Organization (WTO), and with agricultural talks. Ex-EU commissioner Pascal Lamy may have explained that the European Union is always seen as a representative of the above-mentioned values; nonetheless, in the WTO (cf. the Minister's Conference, Cancun, September 2003) the EU plays a role that propagates a neo-liberal economic policy (e.g., liberalization of public services) on the one hand, and at the same time maintains protectionist measures toward its own agricultural sector.

Thus, the role of the EU is rather discordant, characterized by a major discrepancy: most of the governments of the member states are still stuck thinking as nation-states, and therefore do not act as a European whole:

- not as a social union (most recently, for example, in the Kok report on the implementation of the Lisbon strategy, Kok criticized the lack of political will to implement effective measures in terms of employment policies as a general feature);
- not in matters of tax harmonization (which should be based upon necessary expenditures for a functioning and stable polity to cover the basic needs of the population, rather than on the lowest common denominator); and
- not in foreign and security policy, as was made shamefully evident during the 2003 Iraq war.

Ad 4) *Economic integration is not enough to drive European political reform. Economic integration simply does not, of itself, lead to political integration because markets cannot produce a politically resilient solidarity. Solidarity—a genuine sense of civic community— is vital because the competition that dominates the marketplace gives rise to powerful centrifugal forces... The original expectation that the EU's political unity would be a consequence of the European common market has proven illusory.*

I consider this insight to be quite positive: the misconception on the part of some neo-liberal apologists that the market (Who is the market anyway? The market is made up of people and is not a "self-fulfilling instrument.) regulates everything automatically must be firmly contradicted. Markets need controls to do justice to the value of, and right to, the social solidarity people have created. Without state or transnational regulations, values such as solidarity are lost, as "the market" sympathizes at most with the winners. Losers fall by the wayside.

Solidarity in terms of economic integration, would, in my opinion, mean an actual common EU tax policy—key word: tax harmonization (see above).

Political union demands political cohesion, a politically grounded community bound by ties of solidarity.

It is always necessary to add that politically grounded solidarity and commonality are also based on common interests. Pro-solidarity policies function only when a certain amount of self-interest is present. Pure altruism has never really existed—and it is, in personal as well as political dimensions, unpalatable.

Ad 5) Unfortunately the "values of European citizens" are not defined in any greater detail. What are they? The values of the Enlightenment "liberty, equality, and fraternity"? For at least the last term—fraternity—massive changes have occurred since the end of the eighteenth century. Women's rights and equality have become European values, which guidelines from the EU have also helped to anchor the legal frameworks of EU member states (and, as part of good governance, beyond).

Nonetheless, I continue to get the impression (even more so after the 2004 U.S. presidential election campaign) that the conservative side has been the main initiator in the debate over morals; also, that Enlightenment values (those fought for against the power of the Catholic and other Christian churches in Europe) and victories gained against dictators from both right and left, as well as gains in freedom of expression and the media, are threatened in this era of fundamentalist trends that is increasingly evident in all religions. The main issue is: how much individual freedom can be tolerated in an era when the restrictions mandated by surveillance are propagated as necessary for "protection"?

Ad 6) *Where are the forces of cohesion for the new political Union to be found ?*

The longing for freedom, and for security, will continue to grow. With these, however, also the danger of affording priority to seemingly simple solutions—for example, through the dangerous illusion that more police, more military, fewer migrants, fewer refugees, less criticism, etc. equals more security. This can easily endanger the principle of "diversity in unity." Fearful, insecure people seek security—and sometimes traditions and customs can (often falsely) mediate this sense of security, which a modern, diverse, border-crossing world is no longer able to offer. Cohesion can only be achieved through an open approach to differences, and through a commitment to acceptance and tolerance.

Ad 7) The authors unfortunately do not provide an answer to the question, *"What is European culture?"* and do not attempt any definition of it.

The common European cultural space cannot be defined as a counterpart to national cultures. There are, actually, no "national cultures." No one has ever been able to explain to me   apart from citizenship, national sports heroes and historical events— what is "typically" Austrian, or what unites a person from Burgenland and a person from Vorarlberg more than a person from Salzburg and a person from Bavaria. In order to define themselves, individuals combine various components of their identity: gender, place of birth, citizenship, language, skin color, age, occupation, etc.

The only characteristics I would consider to be part of "European culture" are those values defined in the tradition of the Enlightenment that the European Union currently represents.

Ad 11) *Religion was considered, with good reason, as divisive, rather than conciliatory. That may still be the case today. But Europe's religions also have the potential to bring people in Europe together, instead of separating them.*

In times of increasing religious fundamentalism in all religions, it is difficult to see what unifying potential religions might possibly have. Those liberal, open-minded representatives from a wide variety of religions, who in the past often presented a glimmer of hope in the sense of solidarity, appear to have become fewer and farther between. It is as though fears have led to a new moral "hype" of conservative morals and have likewise impeded progressive thought in the sense of letting go of tradition, rather than clinging to the long-established norms.

Ad 12) *Despite this global calling, there can be no justification for attempting to impose, perhaps with the help of the institutions of a common European foreign and defense policy, any specific catalogue of values on other peoples.*

If what is meant by this "imposition" is military intervention for the preservation of EU interests in the name of an alleged solidarity, then I agree and find the statement accurate. However, if what is meant is that the moral program of the EU is arbitrary, and should not apply elsewhere, then I cannot agree. The moral program of the European union is based on assumptions that are founded in multilateral agreements (mainly the United Nations). These have been accepted, signed, and ratified by most nations on other continents—some with reservations, but nonetheless ratified. Quite often civil organizations rely on these agreements— especially those that defend them against undemocratic regimes— and therefore seek the aid of the European Union. Here, global solidarity is necessary.

There is no essence of Europe, no fixed list of European values.
There is no "finality" to the process of European integration.

I agree in the sense that every community constantly continues to change, and is constantly subjected to processes that are prompted and controlled internally, as well as externally. However, we should not make the mistake of believing that what has already been achieved is open to negotiation—for example, when faced with the pressure of fundamental movements, or pressures pushing toward a

surveillance state. Here, what applies for me, and should also continue to apply for the European Union, is: solidarity, yes; restriction of
personal freedom and promotion of a climate of intolerance, no.

This procedural principle also naturally applies to the finality of
the European integration process: even if there should one day be a
political and social union with no nation-states in the sense we think
of them today, even such a construct will be subject to change.

Translated by Dream Coordination Office
(Lisa Rosenblatt and Charlotte Eckler)

MICHAEL MERTES

What Distinguishes Europe?

The powers of cohesion in an expanded European Union must "be looked for and found in Europe's common culture" the Reflection Group's Europe Paper emphasizes. Indeed: "As the old forces of integration—the desire for peace, the existence of external threats, and the potential for economic growth—lose their effectiveness, the role of Europe's common culture—the spiritual factor of European integration—will inevitably grow in importance as a source of unity and cohesion." Whether, as stated at the beginning of the paper, a radical re-definition of the EU really is on the agenda, appears to me rather doubtful—I would prefer to think in terms of an accelerated continuing development of the Union in the light of both old and new conceptions of a final goal.

The emphasis on immaterial factors does not at all imply—as I understand the reasoning of the Reflection Group—a disparagement of material factors. Identity alone creates neither prosperity nor jobs. All public opinion surveys suggest that the citizens of Europe judge national and European policies according to whether or not they are of personal benefit. That is entirely legitimate; it should not be condemned as a symptom of contemptible materialism. Certainly, "markets cannot produce a politically resilient solidarity." But where there is no growth to distribute, appeals to solidarity will meet with little response.

Matter-of-factly, the Reflection Group points out that the ambitious Lisbon strategy of the EU has "been overtaken by events." Indeed, is it not a mistake, by proclaiming large-scale collective economic targets, to pretend to the Union's citizens that there is a capacity for political management that does not exist at all? Unrealistic voluntarism only leads to frustrations, which unnecessarily discredit the European project. Internal European solidarity would be better served if older members like Germany would undertake courageous policies of national reform and face up to competition from new members, instead of complaining about alleged "tax and social dumping."

The space of Europe—according to the Paper—is "in principle an open space," and European culture must not be defined either in opposition to national cultures or "in opposition to a particular religion (such as Islam)." This is also something I agree with. The most important European values—freedom, the rule of law, democracy— are universal, and of no use as criteria of distinction. The Reflection Group rightly stresses that the identity of Europe (meaning EU-rope, to adopt a useful neologism) is "something that must be negotiated." If the term "identity" is replaced by the once popular word "essence," then the full meaning of the sentence becomes evident: the aim cannot be to summon down to earth from the heaven of concepts a platonic idea by the name of "Europe" that has existed for all time.

The crucial question is not what Europe "really" *is*, but what EU-rope *should be*. This is a political question, directed not only at European leaderships and elites, but also at all citizens of the Union. What Ernest Renan said in 1882 about the political identity of a nation also holds true analogously for the *civitas* of the EU: it emerges from "the agreement, the clearly expressed wish, to continue life together;" its existence "is a daily plebiscite."

The issue of future EU expansions, addressed by the Europe Paper with welcome caution, is also subject to Renan's "agreement": "Europe's boundaries too," writes the Reflection Group, "must always be renegotiated." On the one hand, the expansion process is not yet concluded; on the other, neither is it determined by iron historical necessities. In my view, the internal consolidation of a Union that has taken place in Romania and Bulgaria takes clear precedence over further expansion projects, which would considerably overextend the Union's current powers of cohesion. The *"plébiscite de tous les jours"* needs time to allow a more resilient community spirit to grow out of the new EU-ropean diversity.

The Europe Paper mentions Turkey's possible membership of the EU only once, but it is obvious that its statements on the subject of "Islam" must also be read in relation to it. It sensibly warns against "a frontal confrontation between the abstractions of 'Christian Europe' and 'Islam'" detached from any specific cultural and social context. Admittedly, this subject has recently become increasingly explosive, thanks to a series of developments and events. These include the religiously charged political discourse in the United States, as well as the European debate on the limits of liberal tolerance in the face of fundamentalist intolerance.

The conflict, as far as Europe is concerned, is not bi-polar ("Christian Europe" vs. "Islam") but tri-polar. A second line of conflict divides Christianity from a secularism that suspects every religiously founded claim to participate in the shaping of society of being fundamentalist. And, finally—largely repressed until the murder of Theo van Gogh—there is the line of conflict between secularism and Islam.

Within this triangular relationship, a number of co-operations and alliances are conceivable:

(1) Christianity and secularism against Islam;

(2) Christianity and Islam against secularism;

(3) Secularism and Islam against Christianity.

The shared interest under (1) is possible, not least of all, because the Christian churches today accept the separation of church and state as legitimate in principle—whatever the national differences in the constitutional position. They have learned to accept the fact that even critiques of religion that appear to them to be blasphemous are protected by freedom of expression, art and belief. They no longer regard the disparagement of their confession as an offence to be prosecuted by the state, and do not at all condone any kind of religious lynch law in God's name, as exemplified by the cases of Salman Rushdie and Theo van Gogh.

Although a (shrinking) majority of Europeans still claim Christian convictions,[1] Europe today is a "secular universe" (Jacques Le Goff). In Western and Central Europe, there are clear majorities who disagree with the idea "that one has to believe in God to be a moral person."[2] A fixation on the views and way of life of the secular, urban elites in Turkey sometimes blocks our view of the beliefs of "*la Turquie profonde*": an 84% majority of Turkish interviewees agrees that there is a link between religion and morality; in France and the Czech Republic, only 13% do so. In the West it is above all the United States, with a positive response of 58%, that displays a marked pro-religious attitude.[3]

"Necessary to believe in God to be moral?"

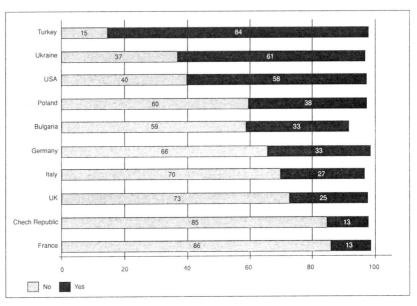

The following remarks by the former Cardinal Ratzinger[4] may be interpreted as an example of a shared common interest in line with (2):

> Secularism is no longer that element of neutrality, which opens up spaces of freedom for all. It is beginning to turn into an ideology, which, with the help of politics is forcing its way into the public realm. (…) In the world of politics it has become almost indecent, to talk about God— just as if it were an attack on the freedom of non-believers… At any rate the firm belief in God of Muslims is a positive challenge to us: their awareness that we face God's last judgment, together with their custodianship of a moral inheritance and the observation of standards,

which show how much faith needs general forms of expression in order to live.

Timothy Garton Ash, a proven liberal, puts forward a similar argument with his warning against an illiberal "secular fundamentalism":[5]

> If the West is split, then the dividing line runs slap bang through the middle of America—and, on the other side of the pond, through the middle of Europe. We [Europeans] may no longer have as many Christian fundamentalists—compared to the American religious Right Rocco Buttiglione, the Italian Catholic who withdrew his candidature for the office of an EU commissioner, is almost a dangerous liberal. Instead we have a growing number of Islamic fundamentalists. And I would add: We have secular fundamentalists—people who are convinced, that a life in accordance with the teaching of Islam or other religions is incompatible with the values of an undivided humanity, and who therefore want citizens educated in that spirit and for the state to pass the appropriate laws.

Finally, in the context of the debate on the possible EU membership of Turkey, there arise shared interests of the kind mentioned under (3). They culminate in the polemical claim that reservations against Turkey are substantially determined by the obsolete view that the EU is a "Christian club."

Incidentally, the asymmetry of Western Islamophobia and Muslim Christianophobia is noteworthy. While in Western countries 18 per cent (Great Britain) to 46 per cent (Germany) express an antipathy towards Islam, in the Islamic countries surveyed 52 per cent (Turkey) to 73 per cent (Morocco) are antipathetic to Christianity. Furthermore, unlike the United States, attitudes toward Christianity in a number of Western countries are considerably more reserved than are attitudes in Muslim countries towards Islam.[6]

The Reflection Group has avoided drawing up a list of European values with good reason: The codification of such values would indeed be "confronted with a variety of diverging national, regional, ethnic, sectarian and social understandings. A constitutional treaty cannot eliminate this diversity of interpretation, even if backed up by legislation and judicial interpretation."

Perhaps, however, a European value system can be defined *negatively*—that is, by way of opinions that are largely rejected in EUropa. The following list makes no claim to be comprehensive; it is based on generally accessible empirical findings:

Nationalism: The rejection of nationalism is the reverse of the readiness to transfer parts of the sovereignty of one's own state to supra-national institutions. The *Pew* study "Views of a Changing World" measures the strength of nationalist opinions in accordance with three criteria:[7] the view that one's own national culture is superior to others; the view that one's own way of life must be protected against foreign influences; the conviction that one's own country has legitimate territorial claims on neighboring countries. "Interviewees in India, for example," according to the study, "agree with these statements in particularly large numbers. The same is true of Turks, Bangladeshis, South Africans and Pakistanis. At the other end of the scale significantly fewer interviewees in Great Britain, France and Germany display nationalist attitudes of this kind."[8]

While 89 per cent of Turkish respondents believe that their way of life must be protected against foreign influence, in the most populous EU states, Germany, Great Britain and France, only 51 to 53 per cent still do so.[9]

"Our way of life needs to be protected against foreign influence"

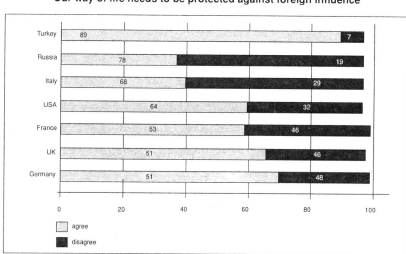

Country	agree	disagree
Turkey	89	7
Russia	78	19
Italy	68	29
USA	64	32
France	53	46
UK	51	46
Germany	51	48

One aspect of the topic of nationalism is also the question of the readiness to openly discuss the darker chapters of one's own national past. It would, therefore, be an important indication of political and cultural convergence with EU-ropa if an open debate on the genocide of the Armenians were to begin in Turkey.

Antisemitism: The *Pew* study "A Year After the Iraq War"[10] also reveals enormous differences between the Western and Muslim worlds when it comes to hostility to Jews. While in the United States 8 percent, in France 11 percent and in Germany 20 percent of those interviewed express antipathies towards Jews, 49 per cent do so in Turkey and in Morocco as many as 92 per cent. In welcome contrast to other Muslim countries, there is a clear majority in Turkey against Palestinian suicide bombings of Israelis (67 per cent); nevertheless almost a quarter of respondents (24 per cent) consider such attacks legitimate.[11]

Family, Women, Sexuality: At the forefront of contemporary European criticisms of the family values of Islam is the lack of rights of many Muslim women.[12] In the autumn of 2004 the Turkish parliament had to take note of the fact that the legal impunity of adultery is an established fact in the EU. Less notice is taken of the fact that homophobic attitudes are incomparably stronger in Muslim societies than in EU-ropa. Only 22 per cent of those interviewed in Turkey, think that homosexuality should be socially acceptable, in Germany and the Czech Republic (the two most liberal countries in this respect) 83 per cent are in agreement. The United States (51 per cent), Poland (40 per cent) and Bulgaria (37 per cent) lie between the two extremes.[13]

One of the foundations of the European culture of rights is the conviction that not the group, but the individual, is the most important possessor of rights. Hence something it cannot accept is for particular groups to claim, in the name of tolerance, an entitlement to deprive their own members of their rights.

Notes

1 Cf. for example, the findings of the "European Value System Study" (EVSS), presented in Hermann Denz (ed.) *Die europäische Seele,* Vienna 2002.

2 The question put by the Pew Research Center For The People & The Press, Washington D.C., for the opinion survey "Views of a Changing World" published in June 2003; see http://people-press.org/reports/pdf/185.pdf (hereinafter quoted as "Views"), p. 115.

3 The following table reproduces only a selection of the findings given in "Views" op. cit.

4 "Gott bleibt am Rand": Interview with Cardinal Joseph Ratzinger in *Die Welt* (24 November 2004).

5 "American Blues," in *The Guardian* (18 November 2004).

6 See Pew Research Center For The People & The Press, "A Year After the Iraq War" (March 2004), http://people-press.org/reports/pdf/206.pdf, p. 5.

7 Cf. "Views," op. cit., p. 93.

8 Op. cit., p. 95.

9 The following table reproduces only a selection of the findings reproduced in "Views", op. cit.

10 Op. cit. (Note 6), p. 4.

11 Op. cit., p. 1.

12 Cf. for example the cover story of *Der Spiegel* (15 November 2004), pp 60.

13 Cf. "Views," p. 11.

ALEXEI MILLER

European Culture, an Ambivalent Heritage

If you ask people who are involved in cultural production where to look for solutions to the problems of integration of the enlarged EU, you should not be surprised if they point at culture. Culture, indeed, should be part of solution. An awareness of some pitfalls that loom in this area is also desirable, however, because culture itself is also part of the problem.

It is indeed impossible to define, once and for all, what European culture is. However it is possible (and necessary) to pinpoint those elements of the European cultural tradition that should be perceived as potential sources of danger. One of these features, for example, is the drive for domination, deeply imbedded in the European tradition. When, as now, the enlarged and, hopefully, stronger EU strives to obtain new power for political action, this danger should be remembered.

Stressing the democratic elements of the European tradition, we should also remember that the word chauvinism has its roots in the name of a European. Europe will shortly and inevitably face immigration on even larger scale, and this danger to her cultural heritage should be kept in mind.

If we say that it is a common European culture that must provide new energies for cohesion and the shaping of a common political identity, we must admit that, as with any enterprise of identity formation, this one must inevitably involve the practices of "othering" in shaping a "we." European culture has a centuries-old tradition of using different "others" for identity formation. As a Russian, I know that this tradition has very little to do with *caring* about the other. (Others on the peripheries of Europe will probably share my view.) All that I know about the concept of Central Europe, so popular in recent decades with some of the new members of EU, does not provide me with much hope that the attitude towards the other and the way the other is treated will change significantly.

The effort to mobilize culture as an instrument for cohesion and unity should begin, not with the construction of a European myth (which is well under way) and practices of othering, but with such values as compassion, self-restraint and recognition, not only of diversity, but also of conflicts in cultural heritage and values. We should remember that when a system of values or a culture are impossible to define, when they are "open," they are also open to diverse manipulations, particularly on the part of those who are engaged in cultural production and equipped for such manipulations. For this reason, I continue to have greater confidence in material interests and in practical politics, where people are more subject to verification and responsibility.

KENNETH MURPHY

Solidarity and Freedom

The Europe Paper is right to focus on culture as a source of European solidarity. Thankfully, such solidarity can be cultivated; it is not something you either have or don't have. Indeed, Europe's history demonstrates how solidarity and national consciousness can arise when nurtured.

It is a historical fact that the tendency towards amalgamation into larger political unions reached its climax between 1860 and 1870. During that decade, Germany and Italy united, the American Union was preserved, the Danubian Empire established itself in a form that lasted until 1918, Canada achieved a federal union, and the British Commonwealth came into being.

After 1870, this movement toward unification was arrested. All true "nations" had, it seemed, been united. But this was a mere rationalization after the fact. It assumed that the amalgamation of peoples into larger unions required national consciousness to exist *before* national unity could be achieved.

But when one examines the pre-1870 unifications closely, one sees that political union often *preceded* national consciousness. Such can be said of the states that forged the United States, of the cantons that entered the Swiss federation, of such unions as that of the Flemings and Walloons to form Belgium. Back then, political union did not depend upon ethnic or cultural homogeneity; on the contrary, peoples of different language, ethnic origin, religion, and history overcame particularism in order to unite.

Around 1870 a centrifugal tendency took hold, and over the next century nationality was invoked to divide, rather than unite. As nationalism was understood before 1870, the movement towards unification had by no means been completed. Political federation of Belgium and Holland, of the Scandinavian states, and of the Balkan states were no more inconceivable than the union of Prussia and Bavaria, of Piedmont and the Papal states, of the Flemings and Walloons, or of Switzerland's German, French, and Italian-speaking peoples.

But these potential unions were not realized. Indeed, some unions disintegrated. Norway and Sweden separated; eight successor states arose in the Danube basin after the disintegration of the Habsburg Empire, seven on the western marches of the former Russian empire. Just a decade ago, Czechoslovakia divided into two countries and Yugoslavia into five, with two more chafing for independence. This centrifugal tendency remains strong even where union survives: sub-nationalist movements are powerful in Belgium, Spain, and the United Kingdom.

Originating as a passion to overcome the particularism of petty states, the philosophy of nationalism during the twentieth century ended up justifying particularism. Where once it ameliorated conflicting loyalties, it proceeded to stoke separatist sentiments.

Although exponents of this later nationalism imagined they were carrying on in the tradition of Washington, Cavour, and Bismarck, they were, in fact, reversing them. The older nationalism reached out for unity among particularists by cultivating a common consciousness, whereas latter-day nationalism emphasizes an exclusive particularism. The older nationalism of 1860–1870 supported political unification; nowadays, nationalist sentiment is an agent of disunion.

The difference is one of inclusiveness versus exclusiveness. Under the older nationalist philosophy, a tenuous sense of common nationality was invoked in establishing political unions. As those unions came to be seen as, and were proven to be, beneficial, strong feelings of common solidarity developed. But there are no guarantees. Witness the anxiety in George Washington's *Farewell Address* over whether the people would ever feel themselves to be not merely Virginians, but Americans.

Opponents of the European Union forget how little developed the sense of national solidarity was when the British, the French, the Americans, the Germans, and the Italians achieved political unity. Seeing the powerful sense of nationality that developed under those unions—indeed, as their consequence—they assume, falsely, that only people who already possess a sense that they are one can, or should, be joined together politically.

This stands history on its head. People can live together politically only if they have a strong national feeling, but the fusion of tribes into nations is inexplicable except on the hypothesis that national feeling develops from the *experience* of living together successfully. By treating strong nationalism as the cause, rather than the consequence, of political union, today's latter-day nationalists promote a doctrine that divides mankind into ever-smaller particularist communities.

Note that the type of nationalism that inspired larger political unions flourished in the interlude before the fall of the mercantilist conception of state policy. The period from 1776 to 1870 was the golden age of free trade and of political emancipation throughout the western world. It was an age when the reforming passion was centered on abolishing privileges, removing restraints, and restricting state authority; an age dominated by the conviction that humanity could achieve its promise through emancipation, rather than planning and regulation. It was in that age of diminishing political interference that so many great political unifications were achieved.

Indeed, the correspondence between the ascendancy of liberal philosophy and political unification, and between authoritarian revival and political disunion, is striking. The question is whether it signifies a real correlation of cause and effect, or is merely a curious coincidence.

This question matters today because enlargement of the EU, and the simultaneous quest for ever closer union, comes at a time when half of Europe has been liberated from squalid, dictatorial regimes. The thesis that the diminution of authoritarian government promotes unity and that its increase is divisive can be fortified by many suggestive historic examples. The American Revolution, for example, took place at the culmination of the mercantilist regime, and the colonists declared their credo in the *Declaration of Independence* in the same year—1776—that Adam Smith published *The Wealth of Nations*.

The American revolt was a powerful advertisement for the truths Smith taught; that an absentee government was exploiting the colonists by restrictive and discriminating laws; that King George III had established "an absolute tyranny over these states ... cutting off our trade with all parts of the world." It was the accumulation of these grievances that led to "separation." Discord among the separated states, each exercising its own sovereignty, led, along with the writing of the U.S. Constitution, to their subsequent union.

Examine the powers granted to America's new national government, the powers denied to it, and the powers taken away from the states, and you find that the U.S. Constitution's authors were inspired by the conviction that a federal union was an escape from the particularism of the sovereign states. They believed that the union could be maintained only if it, in turn, was a limited sovereign.

In the Bill of Rights, which the American states demanded before they would ratify the Constitution, the federal government was denied the powers that were then recognized as the instruments of tyranny. In short, the union was a method of emancipating the people from regimentation by the separate states.

So American history lends weight to the hypothesis that evolving political unity diminishes state authority. That presumption is supported by numerous other examples. Indeed, the young national monarchies in England and France found their greatest support among people seeking emancipation from the intimate tyranny of petty princes and local magnates. Unification of Germany and of Italy marked the culmination of experiments in customs unions and currency agreements that were clear expressions of a longing for relief from parochial depredations.

This is also the pattern of Europe's Union. As the authors of this paper elegantly demonstrate, economic growth and liberalization begins the process of unity. But to assure liberty, consciousness of the need for solidarity must run parallel with a consciousness for the desire for freedom.

ANTON PELINKA

Europe is not Europe is not Europe

The European Union has an ethical quality and requires an ethical quality. The Union is built upon the basic principles of democracy—on political pluralism, on basic rights, on the rule of law. This dimension is manifested in the Union's primary function: The Union must protect the peace—first and foremost the peace within the Union itself. Democracy and peace—this is the mission of the European unification process.

To reach this goal, the Union uses a specific mechanism, which is not an end in itself, but a means of fulfilling ends. This mechanism is the construction of economic unity. The best guarantee of the success of the peace mission is for every single European country to be guided by self-interest in the economic success of all of the other countries.

Economic integration is an instrument that makes political integration necessary. The single market and the monetary union virtually forced the EU to deepen its political system by creating a genuine European democracy. This is the goal that should, and can be, reached by the merger of national economic interests—by creating a democratic as well as a peaceful Union, a factor of stability not only for Europe, but at least indirectly for the world at large.

The EU's democracy is a "work in progress." The Union is characterized by a democracy "sui generis," which is not finalized. Defined by both of the two logics that have driven the EU's development in the past—by the process of widening (enlargement) and the process of deepening (federalization)—the Union has moved far away from its starting point without having made the integration's final stage

visible. European democracy does exist—but nevertheless it is still
developing.

Yet where is the spiritual, the cultural dimension of this democracy, of this unfinished political system called the European Union?
All that has been said—and that is especially linked to the values of
Enlightenment and bourgeois revolution, cannot be exclusively claimed
by the EU, and is not specifically in Europe's possession. Enlightenment and bourgeois revolution are, of course—historically—European (and American) phenomena, but these values have definitely
moved beyond the limits of Europe. What can be rightfully called
the Union's (and Europe's) intellectual and moral quality has been
for quite some time part of a globalized, universal standard.

Human rights are neither a European prerogative nor an obligation only Europe is bound to fulfil. Liberal democracy exists in India
and Japan, in New Zealand as well as Chile—nations that, not even
from the most utopian perspectives, can be seen as candidates for EU
membership.

Europe's spiritual and cultural dimension is universality: the
global values built into historically European values are universally
required and have already been, to a large extent, universally implemented. Samuel Huntington's "third wave of democratization" contains
an especially trans-European perspective, and Francis Fukuyama's
final victory of democracy—declared as the "end of history"—is
focused on the self-evidence of democracy's global success.

The substance of European Enlightenment and of human rights,
as declared in America and in Europe in the 18th century, is their universal adaptability, their claim to universality. That "all men are created free and equal" has something to do with European civilization
and with the secularization established in Europe and America—but
in the meantime those values have become a universal good.

What makes Europe distinct is that it is the cradle of moral uni-
versalism, of ethic globalization. Exactly for that reason, it cannot
suffice to built Europe's identity on such universally accepted values. By stressing these values, the EU cannot be distinguishable
from the U.S., from India, or from Japan. Identity presupposes difference.

Nor can Europe's identity be found without a geographic or a
historic dimension. Without these dimensions, the vision of "global

governance"—that in no way contradicts the existence of an enlarged and deepened EU—cannot be distinguished from the vision (and reality) of "European governance." Without realizing the meaning of geography, why Australia does not have, but Turkey does, the status of a candidate for EU-membership cannot be explained and understood. Without history and geography, we cannot understand (and make understood) that we do not know—yet—exactly where Europe's borders are; but we nonetheless insist that those borders do exist.

The values Europe are and must be based upon are—undoubtedly—part of Europe's heritage. But they are no longer exclusively European property. The world has learned from Europe—and for that reason the difference between Europe and the world cannot be deduced from those values.

The world can also learn from Europe in the future—but Europe can also learn from the world. Many aspects that had a significant impact on the European Convention and the EU's Constitution can be traced to U.S. constitutional history. Many challenges the EU must face, especially in the future—a Union with much more diversity and much less homogeneity than the Community at the times of the Treaties of Rome—can be studied in India: how India deals with diversity; the explosiveness of linguistic, ethnic and especially religious fragmentation.

The quality of European democracy can be proved by the EU's success in diminishing national sovereignty. The history of the Union is particularly a success story because France has ceased to be just France—and Germany is not just Germany any longer. National borders have disappeared and some of the political power has been moved from the national to the European level. The "defining other" of Europe's identity is the traditional nation-state; it is European nationalism.

It no longer makes sense to look for Europe's spiritual and cultural dimension by stressing differences vis-à-vis the U.S. or Islam. Such efforts neglect many aspects of reality—i.e. that Kemal Pasha Atatürk's Turkey already put itself into the European tradition 80 years go; that the U.S. made an essential, even decisive, contribution to the development and the safeguarding of democracy and human rights in Europe.

The antithesis to Europe as it developed after two world wars, after the holocaust, and after the experience with the totalitarian systems of the 20th century is not another world region, not another civilization, not another continent. The antithesis to this—to our—Europe is yesterday's Europe. The spiritual and cultural dimension of Europe can be, and will be, measured by today's Europe's ability to overcome yesterday's Europe. The present and the future Europe must be different from its past. Only then it will have a specific, a distinguishable, spiritual and cultural dimension.

MYKOLA RIABCHUK

Making Barbecue in the European Garden

Ten years ago, *The Atlantic Monthly* featured Matthew Connely's and Paul Kennedy's article "Must It Be the West against the Rest?" with a provocative picture on its cover. A white middle-class American was grilling a barbecue in his backyard while hundreds of colored people of all races watched silently from behind the fence.

The metaphor seems to be highly topical. No contemporary discussion of the future of Europe, of the U.S., of the world, can ignore the profound West/Rest divide that threatens to become even deeper, harsher and more irreconcilable. One need not be a committed Marxist to appreciate Wallerstein's idea of "world-economy" as a highly hierarchical system where the developed "core" nations (the "West") have historically established dominance over the "periphery" and "semi-periphery" (the "Rest"), and where no "peripheral" or "semi-peripheral" nation can get into the "core" without the core nations' support and consent.

Such a view, however discredited by Leninist revolutionaries and anti-globalist zealots, and even more compromised by the corrupted, incompetent and repressive "peripheral" regimes, is largely accepted by those intellectuals who bother to think about global problems. Yet, at the same time, the view seems to be unacceptable for the majority of the common people in the West—not only because of the discrediting and compromising factors mentioned above, and not only due to the apparent absence of any feasible solution. It might be psychologically uncomfortable to recognize that the well-being of the West is largely based on the poverty of the rest; that the so called "free market" favors the stronger player who is in position to establish (and change if necessary) the rules of game, and that the popular liberal mantra of free movement of goods, services, and capitals—without free movement of the labor force—is merely a Western hypocrisy.

Any talks on the future of Europe, therefore, should be placed in a global context. It cannot be ignored—with all its profound divisions and controversies. The Europe Paper marks a rather uneasy path between the Scylla of political expedience and the Charybdis of political correctness. The middle way seems to be simple. The paper asserts that "economic integration ... as a basis of the European peaceful order" is not sufficient today. It requires political integration, based on common values and institutions. Such an integration can be facilitated by a common European culture. The process would ultimately be beneficial not only for Europeans but for the whole world: "To the extent that Europe acknowledges the values inherent in the rules that constitute European identity, those very same values will make it impossible for Europeans not to acknowledge their duty of solidarity toward non-Europeans."

These nice words and intentions can hardly be denied, even though the next sentence presents a possible (and rather typical) loophole for many Western commitments and declarations: "This globally defined solidarity imposes on Europe an obligation to contribute, *in accordance with its ability,* to the securing of world peace and the fight against poverty." (italics mine—M. R.) Double standards that dramatically undermine not just Western impartiality and credibility, but Western values in general, can be easily justified by the notion of "ability." Thus, the genocide in Chechnya, unlike that in Kosovo, could be tolerated; the authoritarian regime in Uzbekistan, unlike that in Belarus, could be internationally recognized; totalitarian China, unlike Cuba, should be accepted; the Russian economy, unlike its Ukrainian twin, could be given "free market" status, and so on, and so forth.

The main problem, however, is that the paper weaves between the apparent task—to support the political integration of the EU (ostensibly represented as "Europe") by a cultural and spiritual pillar—and the hidden desire to represent this particular goal as universal and inclusive. "Fortress Europe" is a reality that will not be dismantled in the foreseeable future, since it corresponds to how the world (i.e. the world economy) is arranged. People within the fortress will certainly benefit from the political integration, and the fortress itself will be certainly more competitive and secure against the internal and external challenges. And common culture and spirituality would indeed be of some help, both internally and externally. This does not, however, mean that—as the paper claims—a solid economy would not

suffice to maintain solidarity within the fortress. The barbecue in the backyard and hungry faces behind the fence may facilitate social cohesion and the solidarity of barbecue-makers pretty well. Of course, a competent politics is also desirable to make the backyard more secure; and a good culture would undoubtedly improve the internal climate, as well as international public relations.

But the entire story seems to be primarily about the barbecue in a cozy garden and throngs of aliens forcing their way in. At least, this is how the majority of outsiders would interpret the ambiguous notion of "European solidarity": "This solidarity must be stronger than the universal solidarity, that binds (or should bind) all human beings together, and that underlies the idea of humanitarian aid." Eurocentrism looms large in the paper and, perhaps, there is nothing wrong with that—as long as we recognize that all peoples are equal, but values are not.

But again, the paper seems rather ambiguous in these terms. On the one hand, it pretends to deny anything like a "catalogue of European values," stating "there is no essence of Europe, no fixed list of European values." On the other hand, it continues to emphasize the importance of the values that European civilization is based upon, and clearly states: "To lay claim to a common European culture and history as the basis of political identity, European political institutions must live up to the expectations engendered by the European cultural tradition." The latter, apparently, not the former, is an unambiguous message for outsiders and an important prerequisite to European openness. Everybody who wants to slip from the (semi-) periphery to the core must accept this precondition as compulsory, albeit not sufficient. A *part* of the former Communist East (but not the *whole*, as the paper suggests) had accepted the rules and been rewarded. Perhaps someone else will succeed as well.

Indeed, fortress Europe is terrible, but it is still the best, the most attractive, the most comfortable fortress on earth. One might not be happy with Wallerstein's world economy but no one can change it from outside, if at all. No outsiders' complaints would be heard inside or, if heard, taken seriously. All these complaints are *a priori* compromised as the laments of lazy bones, failures, or crazy leftists. Sometimes, or perhaps often, this is true. But the West/Rest problem exists, and any attempt to cushion it or, at least, facilitate cushioning—as the Europe Paper does—should be appreciated.

JAN ROKITA

Solidarity under Threat

Whenever I'm invited to say something about the state of European solidarity, I feel the embarrassment of a well-behaved boy forced to do something completely inappropriate in good company: to swear aloud or to unmask the lies of a good and respected uncle. Correspondingly, for some time I have had the strong impression that the idea of solidarity on our continent of Europe serves the same function as the idea of peace did shortly before World War II. The more often politicians call upon it, and the more international conferences and seminars are devoted to it, the less solidarity there is in European politics. Thus it is—in a word—an idea deeply tainted with hypocrisy.

I am incapable of defining the moment at which the anti-solidarity current in Europe became an underground raging river defining the direction of European politics. Perhaps this occurred during negotiations on the enlargement of Europe by ten new, but also poor, countries. These countries, sentenced to half a century of communist occupation, destroyed and plundered by the Soviets and a socialist economy, placed before the Old Europe the obvious challenge of increased solidarity. This Europe reacted with the typical irritation of a rich man who has graciously invited a beggar into his home, and now must incur the costs of feeding and clothing him!

The desire to have a Europe enlarged by ten poor countries, and at the same time, by new and expensive policies in the Union—for example, new security policies or innovation policies based on the Lisbon agenda—and to have this all funded by a smaller EU budget is absurd, and can only be explained by such a psychological state

of irritation. There is not even a shadow of rationality in this desire. And it is hard to believe that serious European leaders themselves do not burst out in laughter on hearing the views they themselves voice.

It is possible that the anti-solidarity current in Europe gained strength under the influence of the deadlock in economic reform among Europe's large countries, chiefly those making up *Euroland*. Certain EMU member states, due to weak political leadership, were unable to effectively deregulate their economies, radically reduce taxes, slow down the development of unnecessary bureaucracy, or abide by the Stabilisation and Growth Pact criteria they themselves authored.

Perhaps ideas from the anti-solidarity arsenal emerged in Europe in reaction to this inability. Most recently, a favorite question posed by certain Ministers of Finance concerns how to force new member states to increase taxation. How do we force the European Commission to protect the national/social goals of individual countries, instead of enforcing the Maastricht Criteria? And more generally: how do we slow down the natural growth of the Community Method in the Union and concentrate real power in the hands of national governments? To answer by reading between the lines: the national governments of a few of the strongest European countries must do so.

In this manner, for example, the Nice Treaty Mechanism was overthrown by the one of Double Majority. Then, there is the threat—it is difficult to say how real this threat is—of creating a Union within the Union of the wealthiest countries just after the EU enlargement becomes a reality. One might say that it was decided that a unified Europe should become enlarged solely because, after the fall of communism, such an action was perceived as appropriate. Then, one might add that, at the same time, the old EU members were likely to avoid the real enlargement.

There is one more factor responsible for weakening solidarity in Europe. It is the desire of old EU members to negotiate freely in regard to external relations. Relations with Russia are at the top of the list. We Poles received a significant warning when Russia limited fuel deliveries to the West due to a conflict with Byelorussian President Lukashenka a few months ago. We—as a transit country and a loyal partner—immediately passed this information on to the Germans. They responded with complete surprise. *"What do you mean?"*

they asked. *"We are completely prepared for this. We've known this would happen for a week."* Another example is the Brussels–Berlin–Moscow negotiations concerning the planned gas pipeline beneath the Baltic Sea.

I have to confess to great respect for the political figure of Prince Metternich. This admiration is not typical in my country, for Prince Metternich played a decidedly dark role in Polish history. In a text written in 1852 the Prince wrote that:

"The greatest gift of any statesman rests not in knowing what concessions to make but recognizing when to make them."

European solidarity is threatened today. I am afraid that European solidarity needs to be saved in the years 2005 and 2006. My political intuition tells me that, after 2007, this will be a much, much more difficult task.

PAUL SCHEFFER

Islam in Europe

In my commentary I would like to focus on the passage in the Europe
Paper that deals in a very general and non-committal way with Islam
in Europe, and the chances and threats connected with it. A subject
of the highest urgency is at issue here; above all since the recent
Islamist terror attacks on the streets of Madrid and Amsterdam. It is
no wonder that attention is currently being directed toward our own
societies. But the grand drama is being played out elsewhere, in
countries such as Pakistan, Egypt, and Saudi Arabia: it is primarily
the Islamic world that is divided to its core.

Islam is finding itself in a crisis that expresses itself above all in
its inability to come to terms with the challenges of modernity. Deep
rifts, whose effects we must take seriously, run through the one-and-
a-half billion-strong community of Muslims. The uneasiness within
Islam has come to us via the migrants, today presenting us with the
urgent question of how an open society should react to a community
in its midst that closes itself off from the rest.

What images of the West haunt the imaginations of the more tra-
ditionalist and radical Muslims? The rejection of the West as a deca-
dent and corrupt form of society has also characterized a portion of
the millions of Muslims that today live in the European Union. This
is a problem that needs to be taken seriously, one gratefully utilized
by populist politicians when they say that immigration is the Trojan
horse of Islam, Islam the Trojan horse of political Islam, and political Islam the Trojan horse of terrorism. Ergo: every Muslim immigrant is a potential terrorist.

The response to this political seduction was weak because the political and intellectual establishment did not want to grant an audience to Islam's liberal critics. These dissidents, who do not mince their words when speaking out about the intolerance within Islam—be they Chahdortt Djavann from France, Irshad Manji from Canada, or Ayaan Hirsi Ali from the Netherlands—are looked upon by many as if they were committing a breach of peace and undermining peaceful co-existence. How this recalls earlier times, when the dissidents in Eastern Europe were accused by the very same social democrats of undermining their policies of rapprochement, and thereby of peace.

Never before have so many Muslims migrated to Europe, where they now, as the minority in a secular society, must redefine themselves and their religion. This is also a new experience in the history of Islam, one that demands a difficult process of adaptation of this religion, which in its countries of origin has, since time immemorial, belonged to the overwhelming majority. For this reason, many Muslims have the feeling that their religion is being denigrated; they simply cannot believe that their Holy Book is part of a plurality of opinions and beliefs.

It remains to be seen whether French Islam expert Gilles Kepel will be confirmed in his theory that the struggle for a European Islam will be decisive for the worldwide modernization of Islam. The big question is indeed what will come after the fiasco of political Islam, which already seems to be failing in its worldly ambitions in Iran. But perhaps it is a form of Eurocentrism to believe that the fate of Islam will be decided in the suburbs of Lyon, Amsterdam, Frankfurt, or Birmingham.

The social effects of Islamist terrorism are poisonous: cultural insecurity in relation to the question of whether Islam can be accommodated in our open society combines with a feeling of general insecurity that has been with us for a long time, one which, in many districts in the big cities, has led to a distancing from the Muslim population. This combination stirs up old resentments that are more and more difficult to overcome.

The fight against Islamist terrorism also presents problems for the Muslim community. What should take priority: loyalty to one's own confessional community, or loyalty to the state whom one has one's freedom to thank for? The rifts in society can only be overcome when Muslims sense that the European state is committed to them, and that they also bear responsibilities. This includes an invitation to take part in public debate and be open to society's influences.

The attacks in the name of Islam are also attacks on Muslims in Europe. They are a warning to liberal Muslims: Look! Your attempts to become part of society will also corrupt your faith. Confronted with this situation, Muslims who live in our society must make a decision. If, as many have assured me, they support this society that allows them to exercise their faith in freedom, they must also engage critically with their own community.

But how much truth can a person bear? It hurts to have to observe that throughout the centuries the majority of violence has taken place in the name of religion, regardless whether that religion pursued an otherworldly or a worldly utopia. We cannot get around this truth. However, a prerequisite for confronting it is the ability to reflect upon one's self.

For many Muslims, accepting that the majority of terrorism today is committed in the name of their religion arouses great difficulties. Above all, they want to protect their religion from all the charges brought against it, while, quite naturally, maintaining that everything good also comes from this religion. As far back as human memory, the house of Islam has been inhabited by violent currents; but this fact is repressed for reasons that, while understandable, have not yet been justified.

What would these Muslims say if the large majority of Europeans held the view that there was no connection between colonialism and a Christian desire to proselytize? If we were to forget the words of David Livingstone, the famous explorer and missionary, who, upon the outbreak of the Indian revolt against the British administration in December 1857, said: "I think we made a great mistake when we traded with India and at the same time felt ashamed of our Christian tradition. These two messages of civilization—Christianity and commerce—should always be seen as a whole"?

What would they say if we bracketed out Hitler and the Holocaust from European history, maintaining, "they had nothing to do with our culture"? What would they think if we said that anti-Semitism had nothing to do with the Christian faith, which, after all, is saturated with the love of one's neighbor? Was it not of fundamental significance that precisely the Germans posed this question?

One would gladly hold up this painful discovery of the truth before all Muslims who rigidly deny that today's terrorism is part of the history of Islam. The French author Paul Valéry, after the catastrophe of World War I, wrote the well-known sentence: "We people of culture now know our own mortality." It is precisely the strength of the contemporary process of European unification that the entire weight of this civilizational collapse is made known to everyone and re-shaped into an endeavor for "eternal peace," as it once appeared to Immanuel Kant.

A crucial difference between European culture and Islam resides in the capacity for self-criticism, in the continuing dialogue that we conduct with one another, and in the consciousness that an open society is vulnerable. Only the insight that people of culture are mortal inspires the search for new forms of integration.

Translated from the German by Simon Garnett

TIMOTHY SNYDER

United Europe, Divided History

In this brief comment I would like to address a problem that arises from a juxtaposition of some of the main concepts of the Europe Paper: how to build and maintain a "common European European culture" despite "cultural differences" dating from the Cold War; how to reconcile the project of "expansion" with the deepening of "European solidarity"? The proposal takes the view that solidarity is a matter of moral positions and positive action, rather than simply a question of the correct redistribution of goods. In this spirit, I would like to suggest a problem and an opportunity for Europeans who are concerned with solidarity: the absence of a common historical narrative in Eastern and Western Europe.

Although it would be difficult to be precise about the connection, it seems clear that the sentiment of European solidarity has grown along with a sense of common European history. In some measure this is the common history of epochs and events that concerned all of Europe, as reflected today for instance in the historical styles represented on European currency. More important, however, is the common history that members of the European Union have made together since the end of the Second World War, since 1945. Although every nation has a different narrative of this common history, it is probably not too grave an error to summarize the postwar West European narrative in the following way: the Second World War taught the lesson that peace must prevail in Europe; European integration promoted both peace and prosperity as well.

What could possibly be wrong with such an account? As with every historical narrative, the starting point is very important. The starting point of this common European narrative is 1945. 1945 is indeed a moment when lessons were learned, and is surely the right moment to begin the history of Franco-German reconciliation, and then the beginning of the European project. 1945, however, means something entirely different in most of Eastern Europe, for most citizens of the states admitted to the European Union in May 2004. For them, 1945 means a transition from one occupation to another, from Nazi rule to Soviet rule. It is the beginning of two full generations of communist rule, which for most people was no experience of political progress.

To begin a historical epoch, 1945 also offers Germany (and in some measure Austria, but Germany is most important) itself the opportunity for a fresh historical start. West German (now German) participation in the European project has naturally involved a particular attempt to redeem the nation from the atrocities of the Second World War. This has involved a special relationship with the State of Israel. During the Cold War, this sense of redemption motivated both Christian Democrats and Social Democrats to pursue an *Ostpolitik* with the Soviet Union and its satellites in Eastern Europe. Now, sixty years later, it may appear to Germans that this work has been, if not finished, at least addressed honorably. Germans, one might believe, have earned the right to treat their history as beginning again in 1945.

Yet few East Europeans can see the matter in quite the same way. After the Holocaust, the center of Jewish political history is now Israel rather than Eastern Europe, and Germany's attempts to pursue a correct relationship with Israel (and with other Jewish communities) have little significance in Eastern Europe. Germany's *Ostpolitik* was not an attempt to engage East European societies, but rather to improve relations with communist regimes. It addressed itself mainly to the Soviet Union and to East Germany. Whether or not this was a fruitful approach at the time can be debated; in my own view, it was on balance the right policy. But *Ostpolitik* simply cannot be remembered, in an Eastern Europe liberated of communism, as an especially generous gesture. The very policies that might have persuaded Germans that they were authorized to begin a new historical epoch in 1945 are unconvincing in Eastern Europe.

Moreover, East Europeans know certain important things about German occupation that have escaped the West European narrative.

East Europeans know, for example, that the eastern front was more important than the western front to the outcome of the war. They know that German occupation policies were incomparably more savage in Eastern Europe than in Western Europe. They know that the Holocaust does not nearly exhaust the record of German mass murder of civilians. No Pole and no Jew, for example, would confuse the Ghetto Uprising of 1943 with the Warsaw Uprising of 1944. This happens routinely in Western Europe. That the French do not know about the Warsaw Uprising suggests a certain limit to their interest in opposition to Nazi occupation. That Germans have not heard about the Warsaw Uprising means that they are unaware that German forces killed tens of thousands of civilians, and then burned a neighboring European capital to the ground.

German historians and German elites know these things, of course. The problem is rather one of general public education. So long as the West European narrative of history remains unamended, the West European public will have difficulty understanding the actions of East Europeans. For example, the Polish choice to join in the occupation of Iraq (which most of us, including the vast majority of the Polish population, probably agree was a mistake) cannot be understood without some sense of postwar Polish history. The communist experience left Poles sympathetic to American arguments about liberation. Likewise, Polish resistance to a museum for German expellees is grounded in historical experience.

In both cases, the absence of a common European historical narrative, embracing both East and West, leads to failures of understanding and solidarity. German and French reactions to Poland's policy in Iraq generally referred to a mindless and reflexive pro-Americanism. In fact, this trust in America grew, understandably, from the Polish experience of the Cold War. One sometimes hears from Germans (including German academics) that Poles are unable to discuss the expulsion of Germans because of a kind of national taboo. Polish objections to an expellee museum in Germany are even characterized as Polish nationalism. In fact, Poles are afraid that Germans do not understand just how widespread expulsions were during the Nazi occupation and the two Soviet occupations. Poles also believe that Germans have not yet come to terms with the totality of events before 1945 that preceded the expulsions thereafter.

The future of European solidarity, in other words, depends on a rethinking of the immediate European past. Without historical knowledge of the East, European mass publics will be swayed by simple arguments flowing from national prejudice. European leaders, whether they know the facts or not, will be tempted to resort to such arguments in a whirl of domestic political competition. Moreover, it will be very hard for East Europeans to believe that they are full partners in Europe so long as their experiences in the second half of the twentieth century are not part of a larger European story. These experiences are sufficiently similar (within Eastern Europe) and sufficiently different (from Western Europe) that the May 2004 enlargement poses a new kind of challenge.

Europeans must find a way to rewrite the larger narrative so as to include both East and West. This requires a confrontation with two basic matters of the recent European past: that the center of the suffering Second World War was in the East rather than the West, and that East Europeans had to experience communist subjugation for four decades rather than European integration. It should be simple, one might think, to accept the full historical force of Nazi and Soviet terror. The European Union, after all, is built upon the premise that totalitarianism must never return. Yet in practice this requires some humility. One often hears the argument, nowadays, that Americans can learn about total war and political terror from Europeans, because they experienced the horrors of twentieth century. This is true. By the same token, West Europeans have much to learn from East Europeans.

List of Contributors

Krzysztof Michalski is Rector of the Institute for Human Sciences (IWM) in Vienna, and professor of philosophy at Boston University and the University of Warsaw. Chairman of the *Reflection Group on the Spiritual and Cultural Dimension of Europe* (2002–2004). Editor of *Transit. Europäische Revue*, Frankfurt am Main, and the series *Castelgandolfo-Gespräche*, Stuttgart, 1985–2000.

Bronisław Geremek is a scholar of Medieval European history and a politician. Member of the European Parlament. Former Foreign Minister of Poland and former advisor to *Solidarność*. From February 2002 Head of the Chair of European Civilization at the College of Europe, campus Natolin.

Kurt Biedenkopf is professor of law and economist. Prime Minister of Saxony from 1990 until 2002; former President of the German Bundesrat. Member of the IWM's Board of Patrons and of the *Reflection Group on the Spiritual and Cultural Dimension of Europe* (2002–2004). Author of *1989–1990: ein deutsches Tagebuch*, Berlin, 2000; *Einheit und Erneuerung. Deutschland nach dem Umbruch in Europa*, Stuttgart, 1994.

Ernst-Wolfgang Böckenförde is Professor emeritus of public and constitutional law at the University of Freiburg/ Breisgau. Between 1983 and 1996 he was a judge of the Federal Constitutional Court in Karlsruhe. Member of the IWM's Academic Advisory Board. Author of *Geschichte der Rechts- und Staatsphilosophie*, Tübingen, 2002; *Staat, Nation, Europa: Studien zur Staatslehre, Verfassungstheorie und Rechtsphilosophie*, Frankfurt a.M., 1999; *Staat, Verfassung, Demokratie. Studien zur Verfassungstheorie und zum Verfassungsrecht*, Frankfurt a.M., 1991.

Heather Grabbe is a member of the Cabinet of the EU Commissioner for Enlargement. Recent publications: *The Constellations of Europe: how enlargement will change the EU*, London, 2004; *Germany and Britain: An Alliance of Necessity*, London, 2002 (with Wolfgang Münchau); *Profiting from EU Enlargement*, London, 2001; *Enlarging the EU Eastwards*, London, 1998 (with Kirsty Hughes).

Janos Matyas Kovacs is Research Fellow at the Institute of Economics of the Hungarian Academy of Sciences and a Permanent Fellow of IWM. (Research focus: *Central and Eastern Europe: Between Transformation and*

Integration.) Recent publications: *Training for the Accession? An Institutional History of Social Policy Reform in East-Central Europe 1989–2002* (with Don Kalb), Oxford, 2006; *Small Transformations: The Politics of Welfare Reform—East and West*, Münster, 2003; *The West as a Guest. Cultural Globalization in Hungary* (ed.), Budapest, 2002.

Jacques Rupnik is Research Director at CERI—Fondation National des Sciences Politiques, Paris, and Visiting Professor at the Collège d'Europe in Bruges. Between 1990–1992 advisor to Czech President Vaclav Havel. Author of *International Perspectives on the Balkans*, Pearson Peacekeeping Centre, 2003; *The Road to the European Union: The Czech and Slovak Republics* (ed.), Manchester UP, 2003; *Le printemps tchécoslovaque: 1968* (ed.), Brussels, 1999; *L'autre Europe, crise et fin du communisme*, Paris, 1993.

Michel Rocard is member of the European Parliament. Between 1988–1991 Prime Minister of France. Member of the *Reflection Group on the Spiritual and Cultural Dimension of Europe* (2002–2004). Author of *Pour une autre Afrique*, 2002; *Mutualité et droit communautaire*, 1999.

COMMENTATORS

Samuel **Abrahám** is political scientist living in Bratislava. Editor of the journal *Kritika & Kontext* and founder of the *Society for Higher Learning*.

Giuliano **Amato** is professor of law and a member of the Senate of Italy. Former Vice-President of the European Convention; from 1992 to 1993 and from 2000 to 2001 Prime Minister of Italy. Member of IWM's Board of Patrons.

Rainer **Bauböck** is political scientist, member of the Austrian Academy of Sciences, Research Unit for Institutional Change and European Integration. Recent publication: *Europas Identitäten. Mythen, Konflikte, Konstruktionen* (co-editor with Monika Mokre and Gilbert Weiss), Frankfurt a.M., 2003.

Jan **Čarnogurský** is lawyer living in Bratislava. A former dissident during the communist regime of CSSR, he became Deputy Prime Minister of Chechoslovakia immediately following the regime change; Prime Minister of the Federal Slovak Republic between 1991–92; 1998–2002 Slovak Minister of Justice. Founding member of KDH, the conservative Christian-Democratic Movement.

Ute **Frevert** is professor of German history at Yale University. Member of IWM's Academic Advisory Board. Author of *Eurovisionen. Ansichten guter Europäer im 19. und 20. Jahrhundert*, Frankfurt a.M., 2003.

Danuta **Hübner** is economist and European Commissioner for Regional Policy; formerly Minister for European Affairs in Poland.

Lech **Kaczynski** is President of Poland; co-founder of Prawo Sprawiedliwosc, PiS (Law and Justice).

Ira **Katznelson** is Ruggles Professor of Political Science and History at Columbia University. Member of IWM's Academic Advisory Board as well as of the Board of Directors, Institute for Human Sciences at Boston University. He is most recently author of *Desolation and Enlightenment: Political Knowledge after Total War, Totalitarianism, and the Holocaust*, Columbia UP, 2003.

Ivan **Krastev** is Director of the Centre for Liberal Strategies in Sofia and Executive Director of the International Commission on the Balkans. He is recently author of *Nationalism After Communism: Lessons Learned* (co-edited with A. Mungiu-Pippidi), Central European University Press, 2004.

Claus **Leggewie** is Professor of Political Science and Director of the Center of Media and Interactivity at the University of Giessen, Germany. Recently author of *Die Globalisierung und ihre Gegner*, München, 2003.

Ulrike **Lunacek** is Member of the Austrian Parliament and Foreign Policy. Spokesperson of the Austrian Green Party.

Michael **Mertes** is free-lance journalist and partner at *dimap consult*, a think-tank based in Bonn and Berlin. Until 2002 he was Editor in Chief and Foreign Policy Editor of the weekly *Rheinischer Merkur*, Bonn. Member of the Board of Directors, Institute for Human Sciences at Boston University.

Alexei **Miller** is Research Fellow of the Russian Academy of Sciences as well as of the Institute for Russian History at the Russian State University, and is Professor of History at Central European University in Budapest. Recently author of *Imperial Authorities, Russian Public Opinion and Ukrainian Nationalism in the Reign of Alexander II*, Moscow, 2000.

Kenneth **Murphy** (London) is a Senior Fellow of Smolny Collegium, Saint Petersburg State University, Russia, and a Director and Editor in Chief of *Project Syndicate*, a global association of newspapers. Author of *Unquiet Vietnam*, London, 2005; *Capitalism with a Comrade's Face*, Budapest, 1998; *Retreat from the Finland Station*, 1992.

Anton **Pelinka** is Professor of Political Science at the University of Innsbruck. Member of IWM's Academic Advisory Board. Author of *Democracy Indian Style: Subhas Chandra Bose and the Creation of India's Political Culture*, 2003; *The Haider Phenomenon* (with Ruth Wodak), 2002, both New Brunswick, NJ.

Mykola **Riabchuk** is a Ukrainian writer and journalist living in Kiev, co-founder and co-editor of the Kiev-based *Krytyka* monthly. In 2001, he was a Milena

Jesenska Fellow at IWM. Author of *Two Ukraines: Real Boundaries, Virtual Wars*, Kiev, 2003 (in Ukrainian).

Jan **Rokita** is a Member of the Polish Parliament and chairman of the parliamentary caucus of Platforma Obywatelska, PO (Citizens' Platform).

Paul **Scheffer** is Associate Professor of Urban Sociology at the University of Amsterdam, and writes regularly for the daily newspaper *NRC Handelsblad.* Author of *The Land of Arrival*, 2003.

Timothy **Snyder** is Associate Professor of East European history at Yale University. He is recently author of *The Reconstruction of Nations: Poland, Ukraine, Lithuania, Belarus, 1569–1999*, Yale UP, 2002. In 2004–05 he was Visiting Fellow of the IWM, working on an East European history after 1948 with the tentative title *Brotherland*.